OK

Chartered Institute for Securities & Investment

Level 3

Certificate in Investments

Unit 7 – Financial Derivatives

Practice and Revision Kit

Syllabus version 11

Contents

ISBN: 9780 7517 9329 1

© BPP Learning Media Ltd July 2011

£35.00

Question Bank

Contents

5
9
16
16
8
16
5

1. Introduction to Derivatives

Questions

1. **Which of the following is the best description of a future? A future is an agreement to buy or sell**

   A   A non-specific amount at a fixed future date

   B   A specified quantity of asset at a non-fixed date

   C   A specific quality and quantity of an asset at an unfixed date

   D   A specific quality and quantity of an asset at some fixed future date

2. **Which of the following is the method for settling a contract for a difference?**

   A   Cash

   B   Exchange of documents

   C   Exchange of financial futures

   D   Exchange of the underlying

3. **Which of the following trades is most risky?**

   A   Long future

   B   Short future

   C   Long call

   D   Short put

4. **Which of the following statements is true?**

   A   A futures contract does not incur obligations to buy or sell an asset

   B   A future is standardised

   C   A future always requires delivery of an asset

   D   A long future is the equivalent of a long put and short call at the same exercise price

5. **Which of the following is the best explanation of the differences between contracts for a difference and physically settled contracts?**

   A   Only cash deposits can be used as margin for contracts for a difference

   B   Contracts for a difference have an interest rate as the underlying

   C   Physically settled contracts do not have interest rates as the underlying

   D   Contracts for a difference are settled by cash, not physical delivery

6. **The writer of a call on a future will, upon exercise, acquire a position that is a**

   A Short future

   B Long future

   C Long physical

   D Short put

7. **Which two of the following are true of European-style options?**

   I   They are only traded on European exchanges

   II   They are traded on European and American exchanges

   III They are exercisable at any time during a specified period

   IV   They are exercisable only at expiry

   A I and III

   B II and IV

   C III and IV

   D II and III

8. **Writing a put may serve all of the following purposes, except**

   A Reduce the intended purchase price of the underlying stock

   B Exploit a neutral/bullish view of the underlying

   C Where a bullish stance prevails and an investor prefers to generate income rather than buying a call

   D Protect the existing stock holding

9. **Which of the following is most true of option exercise styles?**

   A American and European styles only prevail in the US and Europe respectively

   B American, European and Asian exercise styles exist

   C Only American and European exercise styles exist

   D UK exchanges offer only American style exercise

10. **If an investor writes a call, he has**

   A The right to buy

   B The right to sell

   C The potential obligation to buy

   D The potential obligation to sell

11. **If you were to buy a 100 put for a premium of 13, what would be your maximum profit?**

   A 100

   B 87

   C 13

   D Unlimited

12. **If you were to sell a 240 put option for 17, what would your maximum profit be?**

A 240

B 223

C 17

D Unlimited

13. **Which one of the following is false concerning European style options?**

A They are available on the FTSE 100 index

B They are traded on European and American exchanges

C They are exercisable at any time during a specified period

D They are exercisable only at expiry

14. **Which of the following describes the risk/reward profile of a short put?**

A Downside unlimited, upside limited to premium

B Downside limited to premium, upside unlimited

C Downside limited to strike minus premium, upside limited to premium

D Downside limited to premium, upside limited to strike minus premium

15. **What is the profit or loss if the underlying is 95 at expiry?**

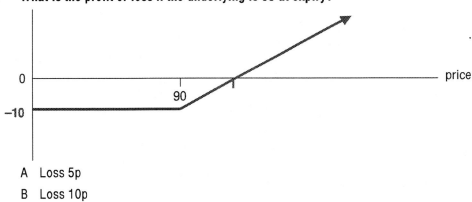

A Loss 5p

B Loss 10p

C Profit 5p

D Profit 10p

16. **The holder of a put option seeks to profit in which market conditions?**

A Static market

B Falling market

C Volatile market

D Rising market

17. What determines the level at which the holder of an option has the right to buy/sell the underlying asset?

A   Expiry date

B   Exercise price

C   Class

D   The Clearing House

18. Open interest is best described as

A   The sum of all long positions less all short positions open for delivery

B   The net segregated long positions

C   The total of short open positions

D   The sum of all long segregated and house positions open for delivery

19. Which of the following is a true statement in relation to exchange-traded and over-the-counter (OTC) products?

A   Both offer formal market places

B   Each contract is individually negotiated

C   Liquidity does not pose problems in either market

D   A formal margining process does not exist in the OTC market in contrast to exchange-traded products

20. Which of the following best describes open interest?

A   The total bought positions plus those sold positions not yet liquidated

B   The total number of sold positions less positions closed out with buys

C   The total number of bought positions minus sold positions not yet liquidated

D   The total number of sold contracts since the contract started trading

21. Which of the following best describes open interest?

A   The sum of long and short positions awaiting delivery

B   The total of all long or all short positions awaiting delivery

C   Daily volume in contracts less deliveries made

D   The difference between the number of long and short positions held by the Clearing House

22. The ease with which a futures trader can move in and out of futures positions by trading on the market is a function of

A   Basis

B   Spread

C   Liquidity

D   Convergence

23. **A naked short call makes money in which of the following market conditions?**

A   Bullish

B   Bearish

C   Neutral

D   Volatile

24. **Which of the following options has the greatest gearing effect?**

A   In-the-money

B   At-the-money

C   Out-of-the-money

D   Deeply out-of-the-money

25. **In the 19th Century, which groups of people were able to benefit from the risk transfer system which was developing?**

A   Farmers only

B   Consumers only

C   No one because there were no derivative exchanges until the late 19th Century

D   Both farmers and consumers

26. **Which of these options have the right to exercise?**

I   Long Call

II   Short Call

III   Long Put

IV   Short Put

A   I and II

B   I and III

C   II and III

D   II and IV

Answers

1. **D** The specific quality and quantity of the asset, as well as exact details with regards to the fixed future date, will be contained within the contract specification. All of these details are defined by the exchange to ensure that the contracts are liquid. If the investor wants to choose the quality, quantity or delivery details, then this would be regarded as an over-the-counter (OTC) contract

    See Section 1.1 of your Study Text

2. **A** A contract for difference will always be cash settled, exchange of the underlying refers to physically settled

    See Section 1.6.1 of your Study Text

3. **B** The maximum risk for a long future is limited to the price agreed. The maximum loss for a long call is the premium; for a short put, it is limited to the breakeven price, but for a short future the maximum loss is potentially unlimited

    See Section 1.15 of your Study Text

4. **B** A future is standardised in its contract size, permitted deliverables, tick size, etc. When an agreement is concluded over-the-counter on non-standard times, it is usually referred to as a forward. Not all futures require delivery of assets as they may be cash settled. We will see later in the Strategies chapter that a long put with a short call gives a synthetic short future not a long future

    See Sections 1.1 and 1.2 of your Study Text

5. **D** A 'contract for a difference' is a cash-settled future. A non-cash deposit, e.g. gilts, can be used as margin for a contract for difference, subject to the restrictions of the exchange. An interest rate future will always be cash settled, but there are 'contracts for difference' which do not have interest rates as the underlying, e.g. FTSE 100 index future

    See Section 1.6.1 of your Study Text

6. **A** A potential obligation to sell the future becomes an actual obligation to sell the future once the call option has been exercised against the writer. This is because the holder of the call will exercise the option, which is exercised into a long future. Therefore the writer of the call will be short the future

    See Section 1.17 of your Study Text

7. **B** European style options can only be exercised on their expiry date. The terms 'European' and 'American' relate solely to style of exercise and have nothing to do with where the options actually trade. Both types of option are traded on both European and American exchanges

    See Section 1.9.1 of your Study Text

8. **D** The purchase price will effectively be reduced to strike minus premium. To protect an existing holding, the required trade is a long put, not a short put

    See Section 1.14 of your Study Text

9. **B** The option style bears no relation to the country in which the option trades. Knowledge of exercise styles other than American, European or Asian is not required for the exam, although they do exist

See Section 1.9.1 of your Study Text

10. **D** Writing a call option (short call) is giving the holder the right to buy an asset. Hence, the writer has the potential obligation to sell if the option is exercised by the holder

See Section 1.12 of your Study Text

11. **B** Maximum gain on a long put = Strike – Premium (i.e. 100 – 13 = 87)

See Section 1.13 of your Study Text

12. **C** As the writer of any option you will only make a profit if the option is not exercised, assuming that a rational option holder would not exercise an out-of-the-money option. Hence, the maximum profit available is the option premium

See Section 1.14 of your Study Text

13. **C** European style options trade on both American and European exchanges. They are exercisable only at expiry

See Section 1.9.1 of your Study Text

14. **C** The upside on all short options is the premium. For short puts the downside is the strike minus the premium as the price of the underlying cannot fall to less than zero. For short calls the downside is unlimited

See Section 1.14 of your Study Text

15. **A** The option is in-the-money by 5p. However, after taking off the premium of 10p, there is an overall loss of 5p

See Section 1.11 of your Study Text

16. **B** Holders also need volatility, but B is the best answer for the put buyer

See Section 1.13 of your Study Text

17. **B** The exercise price is also known as the strike price and is the pre-agreed price at which the holder of the option has the right, but not the obligation, to buy or sell a particular asset

See Section 1.9.1 of your Study Text

18. **C** Either all the longs or all the shorts

See Section 2.2.2 of your Study Text

19. **D** OTC contracts are not generally cleared (and hence margined) through a central clearing house

See Section 3 of your Study Text

20. **B** Open interest is the total open longs or open shorts. Since for every buyer, there must be a seller, if we take the total ever sold and eliminate those which have been offset through a closing buy, this will give the remaining open shorts

See Section 2.2.2 of your Study Text

21.   **B**   Open interest is the total of either all the longs or all the shorts, but not the sum of both

See Section 2.2.2 of your Study Text

22.   **C**   Liquidity in this context refers to the ease with which it is possible to trade

See Section 2.2 of your Study Text

23.   **B**   Bearish/neutral would be a better answer, but bearish is the best available answer

See Section 1.12 of your Study Text

24.   **D**   Lowest premium, therefore greatest percentage return on initial outlay

See Section 2.1 of your Study Text

25.   **D**   Both farmers and consumers were able to benefit from the development of the derivatives exchanges in the mid 19th Century in Chicago

See Section 1 of your Study Text

26.   **B**   It is the buyers of options who have the choice. This is, hopefully, a very easy question and is included to show that the examiner does ask some very straightforward questions

See Section 1.9 of your Study Text

2. Exchange Traded Futures and Options

Questions

1. **Which of the following exchanges does not have open outcry trading?**

    A CME

    B EDX

    C SHFE

    D PHLX

2. **Dual capacity refers to the ability to**

    A Trade in both derivatives and cash

    B Deal in exchange and off-exchange derivatives

    C Deal on behalf of clients and the firm

    D Act as a general clearing member

3. **Which two of the following are features of open outcry trading?**

    I   It should lead to a transparent market with clear prices

    II   Prices are shouted out on the floor of the exchange

    III It enables customers to execute trades for themselves without a broker

    IV   It allows trading to take place 24 hours each day

    A III and IV

    B I and III

    C I and II

    D II and III

4. **Open outcry trading has all of the following characteristics, except**

    A Traders meet face-to-face on a trading floor

    B Bid and offer prices are called out

    C It is a transparent market

    D It is a 24-hour market

5. **The NYSE Liffe financial futures and options screen trading system is known as**

    A WEBICE

    B GLOBEX

    C LIFFE CONNECT

    D FAST

6. **Which exchange uses the SECUR trade processing system?**

   A   EDX

   B   OneChicago

   C   BM&F

   D   DME

7. **Who can trade for a third party only?**

   A   Broker

   B   Dealer

   C   Broker-dealer

   D   General Clearing Member

8. **Which of the following would normally be trading as principal?**

   A   Market maker

   B   Private customer

   C   Broker-dealer acting on behalf of clients

   D   Other

9. **Which exchange uses QUEST trading platform?**

   A   NDCEX

   B   SGX

   C   SHFE

   D   DME

10. **MEFF is the derivatives exchange of which country?**

    A   Norway

    B   Spain

    C   South Africa

    D   Germany

11. **Single stock futures are available on all of the following exchanges, except**

    A   NYSE Liffe

    B   OneChicago

    C   CME Group

    D   MEFF

12.   **On which two of the following are traded options available on NYSE Liffe?**

      I   FTSE 100

      II   Foreign equities

      III   Bunds

      IV   UK equities

A I and III

B II and IV

C I and IV

D III and IV

13.   **On which exchange are orange juice futures traded?**

A NYSE Liffe

B Osaka

C NYBOT

D MEFF

14.   **Which one of the following exchanges offer FLEX options on the FTSE 100 Index?**

A CME

B EDX London

C NYSE Liffe

D LSE

15.   **Single stock futures trade on**

A ICE Futures

B CME

C CBOE

D EDX

16.   **Where is the Bobl future available for trading?**

A CME

B NYSE Liffe

C MEFF

D EUREX

17. **Which two of the following are contracts available on NYSE Liffe?**

      I   Equity index futures

      II   International equity options

      III   UK equity options

      IV   S+P 500 options

A II and III

B III and IV

C I and IV

D I and III

18. **Which two of the following products trade on NYSE Liffe?**

      I   Mini FTSE 100 futures

      II   FTSE 250 options

      III   Universal stock futures

      IV   Individual equity options

A II and IV

B III and IV

C I and IV

D I and II

19. **Which of the following bond futures trade on NYSE Liffe?**

      I   UK

      II   US

      III   Bund

      IV   JGB

A I and II

B I, II and III

C I and IV

D I, II, III and IV

20. **The term EFP stands for**

A Exchange Futures Price

B Equivalent Fugitive Procedure

C Exotic Futures Programme

D Exchange for Physical

21. **Which of the following is not determined by the exchange?**

   A   Strike price

   B   Expiry date

   C   Premium

   D   Contract size

22. **Which of the following two exchanges have common settlement prices and links?**

   A   CME and EUREX

   B   CBOE and SGX

   C   NYSE Liffe and CME

   D   CME and SGX

23. **The following are true, except**

   A   Exchange-traded products are standardised

   B   The buyer and seller of an OTC product negotiate the terms

   C   The individual identity of the counterparty is known for an exchange-traded product

   D   Exchanges offer greater liquidity

24. **The trading system employed for NYSE Liffe equity options is best described as**

   A   An electronic order book

   B   A Kerb market

   C   A Ring market

   D   An open outcry market

25. **Which is the best definition of an order driven market?**

   A   All available orders are on display showing price and volume information

   B   All available orders are on display showing price information

   C   Only market maker and specialists orders are on display showing price and volume information

   D   Only market maker and specialists orders are on display showing price information

Answers

1. **B**   EDX

    See Section 1 of your Study Text

2. **C**   Dual capacity means acting both as principal and as agent

    See Section 1.1 of your Study Text

3. **C**   An open outcry trading system is one where members trade openly by crying out their prices across a trading floor. Customers must use a broker to trade, and trading hours are set by the exchange. Whilst electronic systems may allow 24-hour trading, open outcry trading is never 24 hours

    See Section 2.1 of your Study Text

4. **D**   Only electronic/interoffice trading can be 24 hours

    See Section 2.1 of your Study Text

5. **C**   The electronic trading system used by NYSE Liffe, where all NYSE Liffe products trade, is known as LIFFE CONNECT

    See Section 2.3 of your Study Text

6. **A**   EDX

    See Section 1 of your Study Text

7. **A**   Brokers can deal only for clients, i.e. third parties and cannot take proprietary positions

    See Section 1.1 of your Study Text

8. **A**   The private customer would be acting on their own behalf, but they would not actually be carrying out the trades themselves, so the best answer is the Market Maker

    See Section 1.1 of your Study Text

9. **B**   Singapore Exchange (SGX)

    See Section 1 of your Study Text

10. **B**   Spain

    See Section 1 of your Study Text

11. **C**   Single-stock futures trade on NYSE Liffe (Universal Stock Futures), EDX, MEFF and on OneChicago

    See Section 1 of your Study Text

12. **C**   Traded options are available on the FTSE 100 and UK equities. There are no options on foreign equities or on gilts, although options on gilt futures are available

    See Section 1 of your Study Text

13.   **C**   NYBOT

        See Section 1 of your Study Text

14.   **C**   European and FLEX options are available on NYSE Liffe for the FTSE 100 Index

        See Section 1 of your Study Text

15.   **D**   The Equity Derivatives Exchange (EDX) provides single stock futures on Scandinavian equities

        See Section 1 of your Study Text

16.   **D**   The short-term German government bond is naturally available on the German derivatives exchange of EUREX

        See Section 1 of your Study Text

17.   **D**   S&P 500 options trade on the CBOE. International equity options trade on various exchanges but not NYSE Liffe

        See Section 1 of your Study Text

18.   **B**   Mini FTSE 100 futures no longer trade on NYSE Liffe. Universal Stock Futures are individual equity futures. Although the FTSE 100 option trades on NYSE Liffe, there is no FTSE 250 option

        See Section 1 of your Study Text

19.   **C**   There are no US bond futures on NYSE Liffe. The Bund future no longer trades on NYSE Liffe

        See Section 1 of your Study Text

20.   **D**   The term 'EFP' represents 'Exchange for Physical'. The term used by NYSE Liffe for EFPs is 'Against Actuals' or simply 'AAs'

        See Section 2.5 of your Study Text

21.   **C**   An exchange-traded option will have its strike price, expiry date and contract size set by the exchange. The premium, however, is the price of the option and will, therefore, be agreed between the buyer and the seller

        See Section 2.3 of your Study Text

22.   **D**   This allows for 24-hour trading as contracts move from Chicago to Singapore

        See Section 3.2 of your Study Text

23.   **C**   Exchange-traded products are normally novated through the clearing house or the exchange. This means that the buyer has a contract directly with the clearing house and the seller has a separate contract directly with the clearing house, such that the buyer and seller remain anonymous to each other

        See Section 3 of your Study Text

24   **A**   NYSE Liffe is no longer open outcry – this is now only seen on the LME. Kerb and Ring relate to open outcry trading on the LME

        See Section 2.3 of your Study Text

25.   **A**   On an order driven market, electronic orders are entered by all market participants. These orders will always contain volume requirements and on most occasions price information as well. It is on quote driven markets that market makers and specialists prices are displayed

See Section 2.3 of your Study Text

3. Principles of Exchange Traded Futures and Options

Questions

1. **If the future is trading below its fair value, which of the following trades is the arbitrageur most likely to undertake?**

   A   Sell futures

   B   Buy futures

   C   Cash and carry

   D   Reverse cash and carry

2. **The fair value of a 91-day future on an asset with a cash price of £87 is which of the following? (Interest rates are 10% and storage costs 2% p.a., the market is adequately supplied)**

   A   Indeterminate

   B   £97.44

   C   £95.70

   D   £89.60

3. **All of the following would be taken into account when assessing possible cash/futures arbitrage opportunities, except**

   A   Futures price

   B   Cash price

   C   All option premiums

   D   Period to maturity on the futures contract

4. **What is meant by the term 'convergence'?**

   A   Basis will reduce to zero as the contract approaches the delivery date

   B   The futures price is above its fair value, giving rise to arbitrage opportunities

   C   At delivery, the buyer will pay the original contracted price of the future

   D   In a fair market, the future will be priced at cash plus cost of carry

5. **Which of the following definitions best describes basis?**

   A   The difference between a future's theoretical price and its market price

   B   The cash price minus the futures price

   C   The futures price minus the cash price

   D   The difference between futures prices in different delivery months

6. **The current FTSE is at 4000. What is the fair value of the 29-day future, if financing costs are 5% and the dividend yield is 2%?**

   A 4005

   B 4120

   C 4200

   D 4010

7. **If the future is trading below its fair value, which of the following trades would you do?**

   A Reverse cash and carry arbitrage

   B Speculative trade

   C Cash and carry arbitrage

   D Reversal

8. **Which of the following is the correct formula for calculating basis?**

   A Cash – Futures

   B Cash + Futures

   C Cash – Futures + Interest charges

   D Cash + Futures – Interest charges

9. **Which of the following statements is true?**

   A Basis changes randomly

   B Basis does not change

   C Basis moves in a linear way

   D Basis moves in a non-linear way

10. **What is the time value of the September 101 call, which is 87 days prior to expiry, if its premium is 4.17 and the underlying is 103.50?**

    A 4.17

    B 3.50

    C 1.67

    D Zero

11. **Which of the following traders suffer most from the concept of time decay?**

    A Option holders

    B Option writers

    C Futures buyers

    D Futures sellers

12. **If volatility increases, which of the following will happen to the premiums of options on physicals?**

A   Call premiums up, put premiums down

B   Call premiums down, put premiums up

C   Call premiums down, put premiums down

D   Call premiums up, put premiums up

13. **A synthetic long position is constructed by**

A   Buy call, sell put same strike and expiry

B   Sell call, buy put same strike and expiry

C   Buy future, sell call

D   Buy future, buy put

14. **Which of the following options would normally suffer the greatest daily time decay in money terms?**

A   A six-month in-the-money call

B   A six-month at-the-money call

C   A three-month out-of-the-money put

D   A three-month at-the-money call

15. **What is the likely net delta of a position comprising a long at-the-money put and a short at-the-money call?**

A   +1

B   0

C   −1

D   −0.5

16. **What is the theoretical value of the call on a futures contract?**

Future	= 98.71
Put	= 0.3
Exercise price	= 98.00
Interest rate	= 10%
Days until expiry	= 91

A   0.41

B   0.40

C   1.01

D   3.41

17. **All of the following would be taken into account when assessing possible cash/future arbitrage opportunities, except**

A   Futures price

B   Cash price

C   Contract size

D   Period to maturity on the futures contracts

---

18. **Which of the following put options would be most expensive? The underlying is at 200 and the date is 1 November**

A   January 180

B   January 220

C   June 220

D   June 180

---

19. **Which of the following is false?**

A   The delta of a long call is positive

B   The delta of a short call is negative

C   The delta of a long put is positive

D   The delta of a short put is positive

---

20. **List the time value of all four options (90 call first, 100 put last).**

The 90 call premium   = 15p

The 90 put premium   = 8p

The 100 call premium = 5p

The 100 put premium   = 18p

The underlying asset = 95p

A   5p, 0p, 5p, 13p

B   15p, 5p, 0p, 8p

C   0p, 3p, 0p, 5p

D   10p, 8p, 5p, 13p

---

21. **If a put option has a strike price of 100, a current underlying price of 110 and a premium of 9p, what is the intrinsic value of the option?**

A   9p

B   0p

C   1p

D   19p

22. **A trader is long ten calls with a delta of 0.4. To achieve a delta-neutral position, which of the following trades should be executed, assuming contract size on options and futures is equal?**

   A   Sell ten futures

   B   Sell 40 futures

   C   Buy four futures

   D   Sell four futures

23. **A rise in which of the following will always increase an option's premium?**

       I   Volatility

       II   Time to expiry

       III   Interest rates

       IV   Underlying asset

   A   II and IV

   B   I and II

   C   I and IV

   D   III and IV

24. **If the underlying share price falls, which one of the following statements is true?**

   A   Call option premium falls, put option premium falls

   B   Call option premium falls, no change in put premium

   C   Call option premium remains the same, put option premium rises

   D   Call option premium falls, put option premium rises

25. **When a call option is in-the-money**

   A   Its intrinsic value will be greater than its time value

   B   Its exercise price is less than the underlying stock price

   C   Its holder will make a net profit

   D   All of the above

26. **Which of the following would be the impact on the premiums for at-the-money options if volatility were to increase?**

   A   Call premiums would go up, put premiums would go down

   B   Call premiums would go down, put premiums would go up

   C   Call and put premiums would go up

   D   Call and put premiums would go down

27. **Which of the following is true?**

Share price   = 300p

Time value   = 10p

Intrinsic value = 5p

A   The option is 15p in-the-money

B   The option is 15p out-of-the-money

C   The option is 5p in-the-money

D   The option is 5p out-of-the-money

28. **Which of the following is an out-of-the-money option?**

A   Call option, strike price 340, cash price 340

B   Put option, strike price 2400, cash price 2500

C   Call option, strike price 105, cash price 110

D   Put option, strike price 97, cash price 94

29. **If the underlying stock is trading at 200p, which two of the following options are in-the-money?**

I   130 strike put

II   180 strike call

III   220 strike call

IV   250 strike put

A   I and III

B   II and IV

C   II and III

D   I and IV

30. **The rate of change of delta, given a change in the underlying is**

A   Negative for calls, negative for puts

B   Negative for calls, positive for puts

C   Positive for calls, negative for puts

D   Positive for calls, positive for puts

31. **Which of the following is the best definition of gamma?**

A   The change in the option premium resulting from a change in the underlying asset

B   The change in the option delta resulting from a change in the underlying asset

C   The change in the option premium resulting from a change in the time to expiry

D   The change in the option delta resulting from a change in the option premium

32.   **What is the theoretical value of the put on a physical asset, given the following information?**

Underlying	£112.50
Call	£5.37
Interest rates	6.75%
Days until expiry	78
Exercise price	£110

   A   0.31

   B   2.87

   C   1.31

   D   4.09

33.   **If the underlying share is at £1.30, what is the intrinsic value of a £1.50 call that was bought for a premium of 20p when the underlying share was trading at £1.65?**

   A   15p

   B   20p

   C   35p

   D   Nil

34.   **An investor buys 300 BP 430p call options @15p. What will be the premium paid?**

   A   £45

   B   £4,500

   C   £45,000

   D   £64,500

35.   **Using the principles of put-call parity, if the call premium was priced too low, which of the following strategies would be most likely?**

   A   Buy call, sell future, sell put

   B   Sell call, buy future, buy put

   C   Buy call, buy future, buy put

   D   Sell call, sell future, sell put

36.   **A futures speculator might seek to enter a long position in the market at a level below the current market by entering which of the following orders?**

   A   Buy MIT

   B   Buy Stop

   C   Sell MIT

   D   Sell Stop

37. **The current price for the FTSE 100 Index future stands at 6120-6121. A sell limit order at 6122 may be filled at**

        I   6120

        II   6121

        III   6122

        IV   6123

   A   I, II and III

   B   III and IV

   C   III only

   D   IV only

38. **Into which account would you normally post the trade of an intermediate customer?**

   A   House account

   B   Segregated account

   C   Non-segregated account

   D   Any of the above, subject to disclosure

39. **The Trade Registration System (TRS) is used on which of the following markets?**

   A   LME

   B   LSE

   C   NYSE Liffe

   D   CME

40. **Overnight, a customer submits a limit order which stipulates that ten contracts are to be sold at 17.50. Throughout the trading day, the futures trade consistently at 17.52-17.53; during the closing procedures, the market trades at 17.49-17.50. At what price would the order have been filled?**

   A   17.52

   B   17.53

   C   17.49

   D   17.50

41. **A customer is short ten FTSE 100 index futures at 6150. He is looking to place an order to protect against an adverse movement. Which of the following orders would he submit?**

   A   Buy MIT

   B   Sell MIT

   C   Buy stop

   D   Sell stop

42. **Which of the following is not true of a market order?**

    A   It must be executed at the prevailing market level irrespective of price

    B   It must be executed immediately

    C   It must only be executed at a given price

    D   It must be reported to the exchange upon execution

43. **If a customer has a segregated account, it means**

    A   The transaction ends up separate from the broker's account

    B   The transaction ends up separate from other clients' accounts

    C   Assets are not protected from being used to cover losses incurred by the broker

    D   Margin monies can be used to cover all client liabilities

44. **Which of the following would represent a closing purchase?**

    A   The writer of a call option purchases a call option with the same strike price and expiry day

    B   The buyer of a call option buys a put option

    C   The seller of a call option buys a call option with the same strike but different expiry day

    D   The seller of a call option sells a put option with the same strike and expiry day

45. **An investor wants to sell when the market reaches a trigger below the current level although they are prepared to sell higher. Which is the best order to place to reflect this view?**

    A   Stop order

    B   Stop limit

    C   Guaranteed stop

    D   Sell MIT

46. **Which of the following is the best description of a cross-trade?**

    A   Buy a near-dated future and sell a far-dated future

    B   Buy and sell two related contracts

    C   Take both sides of a trade

    D   Buy and sell within the same day

47. **To liquidate a long position in Brent Crude after the price rises above a price that is above the prevailing market, a trader would tell his broker to use a**

    A   Sell MIT order

    B   Buy limit order

    C   Sell limit

    D   Sell stop order

48. **A trader wishing to do a basis trade on the gilt future has bought a future. Which additional trade must he do to complete the basis trade?**

   A   Buy gilts on the LSE

   B   Sell gilts on the LSE

   C   Buy a gilt option on NYSE Liffe

   D   Sell a gilt future on NYSE Liffe

49. **Where does TRS occur?**

   A   LIFFE Connect

   B   LME Select

   C   NYSE Liffe

   D   LCH.Clearnet

50. **An investor with no position writes a put option. This would be best described as**

   A   An opening purchase

   B   An opening sale

   C   A closing purchase

   D   A closing sale

51. **The process of assignment within TRS is best described as**

   A   The act of giving up a trade executed on behalf of another firm to that originating firm

   B   The act, by or on behalf of an option holder, of informing LCH.Clearnet that an option is to be exercised

   C   The act of executing a trade on behalf of a specific customer

   D   The process by which a trade is directed into the appropriate account

52. **When a firm has conducted a futures trade for a client which of the following must they then do?**

   A   Assign the trade to the relevant client account

   B   Make a note of the broker who did the trade

   C   Record the trade the following day

   D   Calculate the initial margin

53. **Which system is used to report trades and assign them to the correct account?**

   A   Trade Reporting System

   B   Thomson Reuters

   C   MarketMatch

   D   Trade Registration System

54. **Which of the following is the best description of a Give-up?**

   A   An assignment of the trade in TRS to the originating firm

   B   An assignment of the trade in CCP to the originating firm

   C   The method by which NYSE Liffe assigns an option holder

   D   The method by which LCH.Clearnet assigns an option holder

55. **At what price may a customer's buy stop limit order at 20.00 not be filled?**

   A   19.98

   B   20.00

   C   20.02

   D   All the above would be acceptable

56. **What is the system that shows details of all matched trades on NYSE Liffe?**

   A   TRS

   B   DEX

   C   TRAX

   D   CPS

57. **If a trade is entered onto the automated trading system without a specified expiry, for how long will the order be valid?**

   A   Until the end of the trading day

   B   Until the order is cancelled

   C   Until the price is achieved

   D   Until the contract expires

58. **Which of the following must be done by the firm in order for an error correction to be allowed?**

   A   Inform exchange in writing

   B   Inform exchange orally

   C   Submit error correction form

   D   Inform FSA

59. **Using your knowledge of put/call parity theorem, what would be the most appropriate method of eliminating risk in the following position?**

   Short one future, long one call

   A   Buy call

   B   Sell call

   C   Sell put

   D   Sell future

60. **An investor is long the underlying asset and owns a put option on the same asset. Which of the following strategies would eliminate the market risk of this position using put/call parity theory?**

   A   Short underlying and short put

   B   Short call and long underlying

   C   Synthetic long call

   D   Synthetic long put

61. **Contango is where**

   A   Bid prices are lower than offer prices

   B   Futures are more expensive than cash prices

   C   The cash price is higher than the futures price

   D   Market volatility increases

62. **In a situation where there appears to be adequate supply, the market would probably be in which state?**

   A   In contango

   B   In backwardation

   C   Flat

   D   Inverted

63. **The term contango in futures trading means**

   A   Weakening basis

   B   Cash price below a futures price

   C   Inverted bid/offer prices

   D   Positive basis

64. **Which is true of a contango market?**

   A   Nearby prices at a premium to forward prices

   B   Nearby prices at a discount to forward prices

   C   Nearby and forward prices equal

   D   Bid prices higher than ask prices

65. **An investor with no position writes a put option. This would best be described as**

   A   An opening purchase

   B   An opening sale

   C   A closing purchase

   D   A closing sale

66. **All of the following would be taken into account when assessing possible cash/future arbitrage opportunities, except**

   A Futures price

   B Cash price

   C Contract size

   D Period to maturity on the futures contracts

67. **Who is responsible for reporting a trade that has been carried out on LIFFE Connect?**

   A The buyer

   B The seller

   C Both the buyer and the seller

   D The market maker

68. **What is the main source of information for exchange price feeds?**

   A Open outcry trading

   B Electronic trading platforms

   C Position reporting

   D Secondary data sources such as Bloomberg

69. **What is an example of a cash and carry arbitrage?**

   A Buying the short dated copper contract and simultaneously selling a long dated contract

   B Buying tin in the physical market and simultaneously taking a long tin futures position

   C Buying tin in the physical market and simultaneously taking a short tin futures position

   D Selling nickel in the physical market and simultaneously taking a long position in the nickel futures market

70. **How do you avoid basis risk as a hedger?**

   A Roll over short dated contracts to cover a longer hedge

   B Hold the future to expiry

   C Take an arbitrage position

   D Use standardised contracts

71. **Why would a trader undertake a block trade?**

   A To enable them to avoid reporting the transaction

   B To benefit from the exchange settlement processes

   C To avoid anonymity

   D To benefit from arbitrage opportunities

72. **What is the main purpose of the Trade Registration System?**

   A   Matching

   B   Processing the trade after it has passed through the Clearing and Processing System

   C   Calculating margin

   D   To effect settlement

73. **What does a Level 2 screen show?**

   A   All of the orders on the Order Book

   B   The best bid and offer prices only

   C   All of the trades that have executed that day

   D   None of the above

74. **Which of these statements is FALSE about a market order?**

   A   It will indicate the number of shares to buy or sell

   B   It will execute immediately

   C   It will not be displayed on the screen

   D   It will indicate the price that the investor wants to buy at or sell for

75. **A future is trading below the cash price. Which of these statements is TRUE?**

   A   The basis is rising

   B   The market is in contango

   C   The cost of carry is negative

   D   The basis is narrowing

76. **A future is trading below fair value. Which strategy can be used to exploit this?**

   A   A long strangle

   B   A short straddle

   C   A cash and carry

   D   A reverse cash and carry

Answers

1. **D** Buy the future, sell the cash. A speculator would just buy futures

   See Section 1.6 of your Study Text

2. **D** Cash price + Cost of carry

$$£87 + \left(£87 \times \frac{10\% + 2\%}{100} \times \frac{91}{365} \right) = £89.60$$

   See Section 1.2 of your Study Text

3. **C** When assessing cash/futures arbitrage opportunities, both the cash and the futures price must be taken into account, together with all the factors that determine the futures price, such as financing costs and period to maturity on the futures contract

   See Section 1.6 of your Study Text

4. **A** The futures price and the cash price are converging to the same point since there will no longer be any cost of carry at the delivery date

   See Section 1.5 of your Study Text

5. **B** The cash price minus the futures price is known as basis. This should equal the cost of carry in an efficient market

   See Section 1.5 of your Study Text

6. **D** Fair value = Cash + Costs of carry

   $= 4000 + (4000 \times (5\% - 2\%) \times 29/365)$

   $= 4000 + 9.53$

   $= 4010$ (nearest available answer)

   See Section 1.2 of your Study Text

7. **C** As the future is more expensive than the cash price plus cost of carry, you want to sell the future and buy the relatively cheaper cash: a reverse cash and carry arbitrage

   See Section 1.6 of your Study Text

8. **A** Basis is the difference between the cash price of the underlying asset and the futures price. It is always expressed this way round, resulting usually in a negative number (in a contango market)

   See Section 1.5 of your Study Text

9. **D** Basis moves up and down as the prices in the cash and futures markets move according to their own supply and demand influences

   See Section 1.5 of your Study Text

10. **C** $4.17 - 2.50 = 1.67$. The number of days is a distractor

    See Section 2.1.4 of your Study Text

11. **A**   Futures do not suffer time decay. The holder suffers as the time value falls approaching expiry, so the holder can sell the option for a lower price assuming no change in the underlying

See Section 2.2 of your Study Text

12. **D**   All premiums increase

See Section 2.4 of your Study Text

13. **A**   B is a synthetic short

See Section 2.7 of your Study Text

14. **D**   Near-dated at-the-money options will lose most

See Section 2.2 of your Study Text

15. **C**   Long ATM Put = −0.5 (ATM options: delta = 0.5, Long put − bearish, hence negative delta). Short ATM Call = −0.5 (delta = 0.5, Short call − bearish, hence negative delta). This is a synthetic short position

See Section 2.10 of your Study Text

16. **C** $C = P + S - K$
$= 0.3 + 98.71 - 98.00 = 1.01$

Other information is there to distract – it is an option on a future

See Section 2.7 of your Study Text

17. **C**   An arbitrage trade is one undertaken in an attempt to make a risk-free profit by exploiting mispricing in the market. An example of this is the cash and carry arbitrage where, because the futures contract is relatively overpriced, we sell it. To eliminate our risk, we simultaneously buy the underlying asset in the cash market, i.e. we buy in the cash market what we have agreed to deliver in our futures contract. Operating in the cash market will incur a 'cost of carry' – the cost of holding the underlying into the future, such as finance charges, insurance and storage. To work as an arbitrage, the total proceeds of what we sell (here, the future) must be greater than the total cost of what we buy (here, the underlying and related cost of carry). Financing costs and period to maturity on the futures cash contract can relate to the cost of carry. The correct size would not be important as the relative pricing would consider prices on a per unit basis

See Section 1.6 of your Study Text

18. **C**   It is the longest dated and is in-the-money

See Section 2.1 of your Study Text

19. **C**   The holder of the put is disadvantaged if the underlying rises. An easy way to remember this is that bullish positions (long call, short put) have a positive delta whereas bearish positions (long put, short call) have a negative delta

See Section 2.10 of your Study Text

20. **D** Time value = Premium − Intrinsic value

90 call option

TV = 15p − 5p = 10p

90 put option

TV = 8p − 0p = 8p

100 call option

TV = 5p − 0p = 5p

100 put option

TV = 18p − 5p = 13p

See Section 2.1 of your Study Text

21. **B** Intrinsic value is profit if exercised now. This put option is out-of-the-money, as its strike price is less than the underlying. Intrinsic value can never be negative, as the holder would not exercise into a loss. Therefore, the intrinsic value for an out-of-the-money option is zero

See Section 2.1 of your Study Text

22. **D** Long calls are bullish trades with a positive delta, hence the current position

$10 \times 0.4 = +4$

A delta neutral position is one with a net delta of zero. Therefore, the trader now needs to sell four futures

New Position	Delta
Ten long calls (10 × 0.4)	+4.0
Four short futures (4 × −1)	−4.0
	−

See Section 2.10 of your Study Text

23. **B** Increased volatility increases the risk of exercise against the option writers, hence they require increased premiums to compensate. Increased time increases time value. The effect of interest rates depends on the type of option. A rise in the underlying will only increase call premiums

See Section 2.1 of your Study Text

24. **D** The underlying asset has fallen in price so the right to buy it at a certain strike is less attractive, whilst the right to sell it is more attractive

See Section 2.1 of your Study Text

25. **B** If the right to buy is at a lower price than the current market price of the asset, it would make sense to exercise, so we describe it as being in-the-money. The intrinsic value will not necessarily be greater than the time value and the net profit position of the holder depends on the premium paid for the option

See Section 2.1 of your Study Text

26. **C** If volatility increases, both put and call premiums will increase regardless of whether they are at-the-money, out-the-money or in-the-money

See Section 2.4 of your Study Text

27. **C** Options with intrinsic value are always in-the-money

See Section 2.1 of your Study Text

28. **B** Call options will not be exercised (out-of-the-money) where the strike is above the price of the underlying, and put options will not be exercised (out-of-the-money) when the strike is below the price of the underlying

See Section 2.1 of your Study Text

29. **B** An option is said to be in-the-money when it has intrinsic value. The right to buy at 180p when the underlying stock is at 200p would give an intrinsic value of 20p. The right to sell at 250p when the underlying stock is at 200p would give an intrinsic value of 50p

See Section 2.1 of your Study Text

30. **D** For holders of options (which we must assume in the question), gamma is always positive

See Section 2.10 of your Study Text

31. **B** Gamma measures the sensitivity of the option delta to changes in the underlying asset price. Answer A is the definition of delta

See Section 2.11.1 of your Study Text

32. **C**
$$P = C - S + \frac{K}{1 + (rt)}$$

$$P = 5.37 - 112.50 + \frac{110}{1 + \frac{6.75}{100} \times \frac{78}{365}}$$

$$= -107.13 + 108.44$$

$$= 1.31$$

This example uses the above formula since it relates to an option on a physical asset. If a question on put/call parity theorem relates to an option on a future you should use the formula

$$C - P = S - K$$

See Section 2.8 of your Study Text

33. **D** The call option is out-of-the-money, as the underlying share price is now below the strike. The value at the outset of the contract is irrelevant

See Section 2.1 of your Study Text

34. **C** Total Premium paid = Premium × Contract Size × No. of contracts

= 15p × 1,000 × 300 = £45,000

In the exam you will be expected to know that options on UK shares have 1,000 shares per contract

See Section 2.1 of your Study Text

35.　A　If the call is cheaper than it should be, you should buy the real call option, and undertake a synthetic short call to offset it. A synthetic short call is achieved by selling a put and selling a future (or the underlying asset)

$$C - P = S - K$$

$$- C = - P + K - S$$

See Section 2.9 of your Study Text

36.　A　Buy MITs are entered below the current market price

See Section 4.2.6 of your Study Text

37.　B　At or better (i.e. higher) than 6122

See Section 4.2.2 of your Study Text

38.　B　Unless the counterparty had opted out of segregation

See Section 5.3 of your Study Text

39.　C　The Trade Registration System is used by NYSE Liffe

See Section 5.1 of your Study Text

40.　A　17.52 was the bid available on opening. This is better than the 17.50 limit, so the trade would be executed at 17.52

See Section 4.2.2 of your Study Text

41.　C　He must buy to close. Buy stop would be entered above the market

See Section 4.2.4 of your Study Text

42.　C　Market orders are those orders which specify quantity but not price. They will typically be executed immediately at the best available price

See Section 4.2.1 of your Study Text

43.　A　This means that the client trades will be margined separately from house trades

See Section 5.3 of your Study Text

44.　A　A closing purchase is buying an equal (same strike and expiry) option or future to close out a short position in that derivative

See Section 4.3 of your Study Text

45.　B　The stop limit order combines the sell stop with a limit order, such that once triggered the order will not be filled at any price below the trigger, but could be filled above

See Section 4.2.5 of your Study Text

46.　C　Cross-trading involves the firm on both buy and sell sides of the trade to match up with buyers and sellers

See Section 4.1 of your Study Text

47.   **A**   A sell MIT will instruct the bearer to sell at any price once a trigger above the current market price is reached, i.e. it becomes a market order once the trigger is reached. A sell limit order will not sell below the trigger price which gives the trader the minimum profit they desire. A sell stop is entered below the market price to stop a loss exceeding a certain level

See Section 4.2.6 of your Study Text

48.   **B**   There are two different basis trades that a trader can execute. If the trader believes that the basis will narrow, the trader should buy the basis, i.e. buy the underlying and sell the future. Alternatively, if the trader believes that the basis will widen, the trader should sell the basis, i.e. sell the underlying and buy the future. The latter must be the scenario for this question since the trader has already bought a future

See Section 1.5.4 of your Study Text

49.   **C**   NYSE Liffe operates TRS, the Trade Registration System, which effectively prepares executed trades for registration at the clearing house

See Section 5.1 of your Study Text

50.   **B**   Since the investor has no existing position, he is opening a position. The investor is writing a put option, i.e. selling a put option so it is an opening sale

See Section 4.3 of your Study Text

51.   **D**   Proprietary trades (trades as principal) are directed to the house account and customer trades will generally be directed to the segregated client account, unless the customer has 'opted out' of segregation protection. Note that the act of 'giving up' a trade is known as allocation

See Section 5.3 of your Study Text

52.   **A**   Initial margin will be calculated by LCH.Clearnet. Records of the trade should be kept at the time of doing the trade to maintain an audit trail. Assignment is therefore the best available answer for a specific responsibility of the firm

See Section 5.3 of your Study Text

53.   **D**   Trade Registration System is used for NYSE Liffe and ICE Futures trades. The LME uses the LME Matching and Clearing System

See Section 5.1 of your Study Text

54.   **A**   The best available answer since the trading firm will give up the trade to a member of LCH.Clearnet for the clearing process

See Section 5.2 of your Study Text

55.   **C**   The buy order can only be filled at the limit price or better (i.e. lower)

See Section 4.2 of your Study Text

56.   **A**   The Trade Registration System will capture all NYSE Liffe trades

See Section 5.1 of your Study Text

57.   **A**   Unless the trade is specified as 'GTC' (Good till cancelled) it is assumed to be good for the day only

See Section 4.2.5 of your Study Text

58.   **C**   The firm would have to submit the form, prove that it was a genuine error, and show that correcting the error will not disadvantage the client

See Section 4.3.1 of your Study Text

59.   **C**   The existing position is a synthetic long put. Therefore, sell a put to hedge the position

See Section 2.7 of your Study Text

60.   **A**   The existing position is a synthetic long call. To eliminate market risk a synthetic short call is required, hence a short put and short the underlying asset

See Sections 2.9 of your Study Text

61.   **B**   In a contango market, the futures price is higher than the cash price

See Section 1.4.1 of your Study Text

62.   **A**   Contango market is a normal market, also known as a premium market

See Section 1.4.1 of your Study Text

63.   **B**   This is a normal market situation where we have to pay a cost of carry, over and above today's cash price, for agreeing to buy an asset at a future date

See Section 1.4.1 of your Study Text

64.   **B**   In a contango market, near dated contracts have a lower cost of carry so a lower price than far dated contracts. Don't be put off by the unusual terminology here (i.e. 'nearby' and 'forward')

See Section 1.4.1 of your Study Text

65.   **B**   Since the investor has no existing position, he is opening a position. The investor is writing a put option, i.e. selling a put option, so it is an opening sale

See Section 4.3 of your Study Text

66.   **C**   An arbitrage trade is one undertaken in an attempt to make a risk-free profit by exploiting mispricing in the market. An example of this is the cash and carry arbitrage where, because the futures contract is relatively overpriced, we sell it. To eliminate our risk, we simultaneously buy the underlying asset in the cash market, i.e. we buy in the cash market what we have agreed to deliver in our futures contract. Operating in the cash market will incur a 'cost of carry' – the costs of holding the underlying into the future, such as finance charges, insurance and storage. To work as an arbitrage, the total proceeds of what we sell (here, the future) must be greater than the total cost of what we buy (here, the underlying and related costs of carry). Financing costs and period to maturity on the futures contract relate to the costs of carry. The contract size would not be important as the relative pricing would consider prices on a per unit basis

See Section 1.6 of your Study Text

67. **C** The system will automatically report the trade for both buyers and sellers

See Section 3 of your Study Text

68. **B** Information from electronic trading platforms will provide the majority of the data

See Section 3.1.3 of your Study Text

69. **C** Remember that for an arbitrage trade we need to be long in one market and short in the other. The cash and carry arbitrage involves buying in the cash market and carrying the asset, whilst agreeing to sell it in the futures market. It is undertaken when the futures price is judged to be above the fair value

See Section 1.6 of your Study Text

70. **B** Basis risk occurs when the movement in the hedging instrument does not match the commodity being hedged. If the future is held to maturity, there is no basis risk due to the process of convergence

See Section 1.5.2 of your Study Text

71. **B** A block trade is negotiated off the exchange in a bilateral manner. But the settlement is through the exchange systems, thus providing comfort to the two counterparties

See Section 3.1.1 of your Study Text

72. **A** In reality TRS has a very limited role these days since most trades are executed on electronic systems and are, therefore, automatically matched

See Section 5.1 of your Study Text

73. **A** The Level 2 screen shows market depth. It is the Level 1 screen that shows the best bid and offer prices

See Section 4.2.2 of your Study Text

74. **D** Market orders are 'at best' orders and do not indicate a price. All other answers are correct

See Section 4.2.1 of your Study Text

75. **C** The market is in backwardation when futures are trading below the cash price. The basis could be rising or narrowing but we don't know this with any certainty

See Section 1.4 of your Study Text

76. **D** The message is 'buy what is cheap, sell what is expensive'. In this case, since the future is trading below fair value we would buy it. Consequently we would sell the cash and crystallise the profit when price correction occurs. Selling the cash asset and buying the future is a reverse cash and carry

See Section 1.6 of your Study Text

4. Principles of OTC Derivatives

Questions

1. **You buy a receiver swaption. What are you hedging against?**

    A   An increased credit spread

    B   A rising interest rate

    C   A falling interest rate

    D   A steepening yield curve

2. **Which one of the following is a credit derivative?**

    A   Total return swap

    B   Asset swap

    C   Interest rate swap

    D   Basis swap

3. **What happens when a bond is suddenly downgraded?**

    A   The price falls to zero

    B   The price falls and the yield falls

    C   The price falls and the yield rises

    D   The price falls and the yield stays the same

4. **What is the name for the start date of an interest rate swap?**

    A   Opening date

    B   Effective date

    C   Initiation date

    D   Take up date

5. **What does the term '2 v 5' mean in relation to a forward rate agreement (FRA)?**

    A   The FRA will start in two months' time and end five months after it has started

    B   One party agrees to pay 2% above LIBOR in return for a fixed 5% interest rate

    C   The FRA will exchange fixed rate interest for two months followed by floating rate interest for five months

    D   The FRA will start in two months' time from today and end in five months' time from today

6. **Which of the following is the best description of a swaption?**

    A   An agreement to buy or sell a swap agreement for an agreed price

    B   An option to enter into an exchange-traded contract for difference

    C   An agreement to enter into an exchange-traded contract for difference

    D   An option to enter into a swap agreement for an agreed price

7. **Which of the following is TRUE of term sheets?**

    A   They must be copied to the regulator

    B   They must be exchanged with the counterparty

    C   They must be matched with the trade system

    D   They are secondary to the Master Agreement

8. **What are the receipt and payment obligations of an investor in a total return swap?**

    A   Pay increase in share price; pay dividend; receive floating rate

    B   Receive increase in share price; receive dividend; pay floating rate

    C   Pay increase in share price; receive dividend; receive floating rate

    D   Receive increase in shares; pay dividend; pay floating rate

9. **What is the best definition of a 2v5 FRA?**

    A   A forward on an interest rate where the buyer of the FRA pays the seller the difference between the FRA rate and three-month LIBOR in two months' time if interest rates rise

    B   A forward on an interest rate where the buyer of the FRA pays the seller the difference between the FRA rate and three-month LIBOR in two months' time if interest rates fall

    C   A forward on an interest rate where the buyer of the FRA pays the seller the difference between the FRA rate and three-month LIBOR in five months' time if interest rates rise

    D   A forward on an interest rate where the buyer of the FRA pays the seller the difference between the FRA rate and three-month LIBOR in five months' time if interest rates fall

10. **Which of the following is TRUE of an interest rate swap?**

    The life of a swap is between its

    A   Trade Date and Termination Date

    B   Effective Date and Termination Date

    C   Exercise Date and Termination Date

    D   Reset Date and Termination Date

11. **What is the correct order in an OTC transaction?**

    A   Reconciliation, settlement, verification

    B   Verification, settlement, reconciliation

    C   Verification, reconciliation, settlement

    D   Reconciliation, verification, settlement

12. **What is the best definition of a credit line?**

   A   Policy of credit management

   B   The credit issued to a client

   C   A percentage of the credit issued to a client

   D   The firms initial margin requirement

13. **What is a rollercoaster swap?**

   A   A swap where the notional principal is adjusted according to prevailing market conditions

   B   A swap where the notional principal is adjusted in line with seasonal requirements as agreed at the outset

   C   A swap in which the notional principle reduces over time

   D   A swap in which the notional principle increases over time

14. **In which one of the following strategies does the buyer also sell an option to the seller?**

   A   A straddle

   B   A strangle

   C   A collar

   D   A swaption

15. **Why did the OTC market develop?**

   A   To provide liquidity to market participants

   B   To promote standardisation of derivatives contracts

   C   To provide retail investors with better access to derivative products

   D   To allow accurate hedging of positions

16. **Which ONE of the following would be the main benefit following the implementation of straight-through processing?**

   A   Reduced capital adequacy requirement

   B   Increased regulatory reporting ability

   C   Reduced operational costs

   D   Increased settlement ability

17. **How are obligations under a forward contract usually closed out?**

   A   By agreement with the original counterparty to the trade

   B   By entering into an equal and offsetting trade with another counterparty

   C   Through the exchange

   D   By net cash settlement via the clearing house

18. **What is the implication of having a Master Agreement?**

    A   There is no need for a trade confirmation

    B   The Master Agreement takes precedence over the specific information in the confirmation

    C   Netting terms are excluded as these are dealt with in a separate legal document

    D   There needs to be less information in the confirmation

19. **Normal settlement of the option premium occurs by when it OTC contracts?**

    A   T + 2

    B   T + 3

    C   T + 4

    D   There is no assumed settlement term

20. **What is actually swapped in a commodity swap?**

    A   The physical commodity for a floating cash payment

    B   The physical commodity for a fixed cash payment

    C   The net of a floating payment linked to the commodity price and a fixed price

    D   A floating interest rate for a fixed interest rate

21. **In the context of OTC settlement, what is the purpose of a bridge?**

    A   To enable the cross-border trading of emissions contracts

    B   To establish bilateral mark to market arrangements for collateral

    C   To avoid 'bear squeezes'

    D   To achieve cross-product netting

Answers

1. **C**   You have bought the right to receive a predetermined fixed rate in an interest rate swap at a future date and to pay LIBOR. You will benefit if interest rates fall. This strategy protects savers

    See Section 1.4 of your Study Text

2. **A**   A total return swap will exchange the total return on an asset against a fixed return and thus will include price movements due to credit events

    See Section 1.7 of your Study Text

3. **C**   A downgrade in the credit rating of a bond signals an increase in the default risk. The price falls and because of the inverse relationship between prices and yields the yield will rise

    See Section 1.9 of your Study Text

4. **B**   The start and end dates of a swap are known as the effective and termination dates respectively

    See Section 1.4.1 of your Study Text

5. **D**   The convention for Forward Rate Agreements is to give the starting month and ending month all based on today's date

    See Section 1.2 of your Study Text

6. **D**   As an option, this will give the right, not an agreement or obligation, to enter into a swap. Swaps are OTC products

    See Section 1.4.2 of your Study Text

7. **B**   The confirmation contains the terms and conditions of the trade and is also referred to as a term sheet

    See Section 2.3 of your Study Text

8. **B**   Here it is assumed that the 'investor' is buying the 'total return'

    See Section 1.7 of your Study Text

9. **B**   A 2v5 FRA refers to a Forward Rate Agreement on a LIBOR rate that starts two months from now and ends five months from now, i.e. 3 month LIBOR. The buyer of an FRA pays the fixed rate and therefore profits if rates rise, and makes a cash payment to the seller if rates fall. The payment is made at the beginning of the period to which LIBOR rates (i.e. in two months) and not at the end as is the case with an interest rate swap. The cash flow will be the net present value of the difference in the two interests rates. (You are not required to know how to calculate this)

    See Section 1.2 of your Study Text

10 **B**   These are the terms used in the market. It is important to learn them

    See Section 1.4.1 of your Study Text

11. **B** Verification of the trade confirmation, settlement of the trade, reconciliation of amounts received and paid

See Section 6 of your Study Text

12. **B** This is the basic definition of a credit line

See Section 6.8 of your Study Text

13. **B** Make sure that you learn about the different types of swaps. The examiner often asks about accreting (where the notional rises over time) and amortising (where the notional falls over time)

See Section 3.4 of your Study Text

14. **C** A collar is the buying of a cap (calls on an FRA) and selling of a floor (puts on an FRA) for a borrower or the reverse for a depositor

See Section 1.3 of your Study Text

15. **D** Answers A to C are advantages of exchange-traded markets and help explain their explosive growth

See Section 1 of your Study Text

16. **C** Again the implementation of STP will have knock on effects such as increased settlement ability but the main purpose is the drive to lower costs

See Section 6.7 of your Study Text

17. **A** If the investor takes out an opposite contract with another counterparty this will achieve the desired aim, but with additional credit risk as forwards are OTC products without a central counterparty. The most common method would be to offset with the original counterparty and make/receive a cash payment based on the value of the underlying

See Section 1.1 of your Study Text

18. **D** The confirmation will not need to contain all of the issues dealt with in the Master Agreement

See Section 2.3 of your Study Text

19. **A** T + 2 at the latest is the accepted benchmark

See Section 5.5 of your Study Text

20. **C** The assumption for commodity swaps is that they are not physically settled

See Section 1.7 of your Study Text

21. **D** Bridges allows cross product netting to be brought into an existing ISDA Master Agreement without the need for separate negotiation

See Section 6.8 of your Study Text

5. Principles of Clearing and Margin

Questions

1. **Which two of the following are covered by the LCH.Clearnet guarantee?**

   I   FSA Authorised firms

   II   NYSE Liffe Clearing Members

   III LME Ring Members

   IV   NYSE Liffe Non-clearing Members

   A I and III

   B II and III

   C II and IV

   D III and IV

2. **An investor goes long four December Long Gilt futures and long two March Long Gilt futures. Which of the following is true of initial margin?**

   A Initial margin will be lowered as the two trades offset each other partially

   B There will be no effect on initial margin as the two trades do not offset each other

   C There will be additional initial margin to pay over and above the normal initial margins due to the concentration of risk

   D There will be no initial margin payable on either trade as they completely offset each other

3. **The procedure by which the clearing house becomes the principal to the contract is known as**

   A Confirmation

   B Assignment

   C Novation

   D Allocation

4. **Which of the following best describes the relationship of LCH.Clearnet with its clearing members?**

   A Principal to broker

   B Principal to client

   C Broker to broker

   D Principal to principal

5.   Which of the following trades is not necessarily a contingent liability transaction?

A   Long call

B   Long future

C   Short call

D   Short future

---

6.   Which two of the following statements are true in respect of transactions cleared by LCH.Clearnet?

I   LCH.Clearnet stands as principal to both buyer and seller

II   LCH.Clearnet guarantees performance of the contract

III   LCH.Clearnet guarantees that a member firm will not default

IV   LCH.Clearnet guarantees contracts to segregated customers

A   I and II

B   II and III

C   I and III

D   II and IV

---

7.   What is the name of the system used to calculate initial margin by LCH.Clearnet?

A   CONNECT

B   CREST

C   London SPAN

D   CTD

---

8.   A private investor places an order with his futures broker. Where is his credit risk?

A   The Exchange member with whom the futures broker placed the deal

B   LCH.Clearnet

C   The futures broker

D   The FSA

---

9.   Who must pay initial margin?

A   Option seller closing a position

B   Option buyer and seller

C   Option buyer

D   Option writer

---

10.   Which of the following is an RCH?

A   NYSE Liffe

B   OCC

C   LCH.Clearnet

D   ICE Futures

11. **Which of the following is likely to occur if a clearing member builds up too great an exposure?**

    A LCH.Clearnet will offset their position with another clearing member

    B LCH.Clearnet will instruct the clearing member to reduce their exposure

    C Under the mutual guarantee system, other clearing members will take on some of the risk

    D The FSA will take appropriate disciplinary measures

12. **Which of the following is an example of a clearing house incorporated as a company?**

    A LCH.Clearnet

    B NYSE Liffe

    C CME

    D SWX Europe

13. **Which of the following is true of margin requirements calculated by SPAN for a portfolio?**

    A All positions will be margined individually

    B Margin calculations account for the offsetting of positions within the portfolio

    C Only long positions will be margined within the portfolio

    D Only variation margin will be payable for portfolio positions

14. **The guarantee offered by LCH.Clearnet extends to which of the following?**

    A Clearing Members

    B General Clearing Members

    C Brokers

    D Customers

15. **At what point does LCH.Clearnet become the legal counterparty to a trade?**

    A On registration of the trade through TRS

    B On matching of the trade on LIFFE CONNECT

    C On verbal agreement of the trade in open outcry trades

    D On payment of initial margin in acceptable collateral to LCH.Clearnet

16. **Which one of the following is true?**

    A The customer's margin requirements are calculated by LCH.Clearnet

    B Brokers must call the full margin as calculated by SPAN from their customers

    C Initial margin must be paid in cash

    D Variation margins can be in cash or non-cash assets which may be subject to a haircut

17. When must an intraday margin be paid?

A   Immediately

B   By 12:00 the same day

C   By 09:00 the next day

D   By the end of the day

18. What is the relationship between LCH.Clearnet and its clearing members?

A   Principal to Agent

B   Agent to Agent

C   Principal to Principal

D   Agent to Principal

19. What is the best description of the system by which clearing members of LCH.Clearnet have an obligation to contribute if a member defaults?

A   Independent guarantee

B   Members Default Fund

C   Exchange-based guarantee

D   Mutual guarantee

20. Which of the following statements is false in respect of maintenance margin?

A   It is another name for variation margin

B   It is a system of margining operated by a number of derivative exchanges, particularly in the US

C   When an account falls to the maintenance margin level, it must be replenished by the customer up to the previous maximum balance on the account

D   Maintenance margin arrangements can be operated in the UK between brokers and their customers

21. Which statement best describes SPAN margin?

A   Maximum close out cost of a defaulting member's position

B   Maximum close out cost of any individual position of a defaulting member

C   Minimum close out cost of a defaulting member's position

D   Minimum close out cost of any individual position of a defaulting member

22. What is a feature of London SPAN using net Liquidation Value?

A   No margin is due on purchased options

B   It calculates initial margin for purchased options

C   It automatically liquidates options which are in the money

D   It only charges margin on out-of-the-money options

23. **In which market do price limits occasionally operate for the JGB future?**

    A   ICE Futures

    B   NYSE Liffe

    C   LME

    D   EDX

24. **What is the best definition of clearing?**

    A   Recording and matching trades and maintaining positions

    B   Ensuring legal obligations resulting from a trade are met

    C   Continuous trading activity throughout the trading day

    D   Using derivatives that will be physically delivered

25. **Which of the following is acceptable for initial margin?**

    A   T-bills

    B   Japanese bonds

    C   German shares

    D   Norwegian bonds

26. **In respect of a single trade, which of the following will take place at the latest chronological stage?**

    A   Allocation of a transaction number to the deal

    B   Return of initial margin

    C   Settlement of variation margin

    D   Filling the order which was GTC

27. **An investor goes into some short option contracts on NYSE Liffe. What is paid?**

    A   The net of the premium and initial margin, paid on trade date

    B   The net of the premium and initial margin, paid one business day after the trade date

    C   The premium and initial margin, paid on the trade date

    D   The premium and initial margin, paid one business day after the trade date

28. **What is the aim of a position limit?**

    A   To reduce volatility

    B   To discourage market manipulation

    C   To encourage competition

    D   To facilitate trade reporting

29. **Why would a client pay variation margin to her broker?**

A Interest is charged on unpaid margin balances

B Interest is charged on unpaid margin balances after five business days

C If the margin is not paid within five business days her position would be closed out and she would face an unlimited loss

D If the margin is not paid within five business days her position would be closed out and she would face a limited loss

30. **For what type of transaction may a firm pay margin monies out of the house account?**

A Client trades

B Proprietary trades

C Both proprietary and client trades

D Internal transfers only

31. **What is a prime broker obliged to provide for its clients?**

A Lending facilities

B Office space

C Global settlement

D Best execution

32. **What is another name for counterparty risk?**

A Liquidity risk

B Novation risk

C Credit risk

D Exchange risk

33. **When does LCH.Clearnet assume the role of the central counterparty?**

A When an order is placed

B When a trade is agreed

C When a trade is reported

D When a trade is matched

34. **When will LCH.Clearnet call for intra day margin?**

A When a block trade has been agreed

B When trading has been temporarily halted

C When there is a volatility shock

D When there is an exceptional amount of trading activity

35. **Which type of exchange member is able to clear trades for non-clearing members?**

A Individual clearing members

B General clearing members

C All exchange members

D Market makers only

---

36. **In the context of margin for intra market and inter market spreads, which of these statements is TRUE?**

A Neither benefit from reduced margin

B Both benefit equally from reduced margin

C Intra market spreads will generally benefit more than inter market spreads

D Inter market spreads will generally benefit more than intra market spreads

---

37. **What is the best definition of clearing?**

A Registering the trades and managing positions

B Ensuring the settlement process

C Managing the trading process and the matching of the trade

D Providing best execution for all trades

Answers

1. **B**   LME Ring Members are always LCH.Clearnet clearing members. Only clearing members are covered directly by the LCH.Clearnet guarantee

    See Section 1.3 of your Study Text

2. **B**   Both trades involve buying futures so there is no offset and both will pay initial margin

    See Section 2.1 of your Study Text

3. **C**   Novation is the name of the process whereby the clearing house becomes buyer to every seller and seller to every buyer

    See Sections 1.2 of your Study Text

4. **D**   LCH.Clearnet deals with its clearing members as principal to principal due to the process of novation

    See Section 1.2 of your Study Text

5. **A**   A long call option could potentially have the premium paid immediately, also known as 'upfront'. If this is the case, the maximum loss, the premium, has already been paid and, therefore, there can be no further losses or additional sums payable. Therefore, the best answer is the long call option. Long and short futures, in addition to short call options, require margining, hence these are examples of a contingent liability transaction

    See Section 2.5.1 of your Study Text

6. **A**   Trades cleared by LCH.Clearnet are novated such that LCH.Clearnet itself becomes the legal counterparty to both buyer and seller. LCH.Clearnet then guarantees each of these two contracts (LCH.Clearnet/Buyer, LCH.Clearnet/Seller). However, the guarantee only protects the firms that are clearing members of the exchanges. Underlying customers who are not clearing members are not protected and LCH.Clearnet cannot guarantee that a firm will not default

    See Sections 1.1 of your Study Text

7. **C**   The system used to calculate initial margin by LCH.Clearnet is London SPAN, which is an acronym for Standard Portfolio Analysis of Risk

    See Section 2.1.1 of your Study Text

8. **C**   The private investor is at risk if his broker defaults. The LCH.Clearnet guarantee only protects clearing members of exchanges

    See Section 1.3 of your Study Text

9. **D**   Option buyers would pay initial margin if the premium was payable on close and not upfront

    See Section 2.5.1 of your Study Text

10. **C**   RCH is an abbreviation of Recognised Clearing House

    See Section 1.1.2 of your Study Text

11. **B** One of the roles of LCH.Clearnet is to monitor the positions taken by its clearing members. They will instruct a member to reduce their positions if considered excessive

See Section 1.5 of your Study Text

12. **A** LCH.Clearnet is the main clearing house for the London markets. It is incorporated as a company. All the other options are exchanges

See Section 1.4 of your Study Text

13. **B** LCH.Clearnet operates a net clearing structure where positions within a portfolio may be offset to reduce the total margin payable

See Section 1.4 of your Study Text

14. **A** It extends to all clearing members, both general and individual

See Section 1.3 of your Study Text

15. **A** The process of registration is when LCH.Clearnet becomes the legal counterparty to all trades through the process of novation

See Section 1.2 of your Study Text

16. **B** LCH.Clearnet directly margins only its clearing members, who must in turn call at least the SPAN margin from their customers. Variation margins must be paid in cash, but initial margin payments can be paid using collateral

See Section 2.4 of your Study Text

17. **A** Intraday margin is called in highly volatile market conditions, when the 'worst probable one day loss' as calculated by SPAN and taken in the form of initial margin, is not considered sufficient to cover the day's risk. Given that such conditions can occur at any time during the day, there is no set time when intraday margin is payable

See Sections 2.5 of your Study Text

18. **C** Through the process of novation, LCH.Clearnet becomes the buyer to every seller and the seller to every buyer. Thus they deal with the clearing members as 'Principal to Principal'

See Section 1.2 of your Study Text

19. **D** LCH.Clearnet operates a mutual guarantee where, once the initial margin and other resources of the defaulting member have been used up, LCH.Clearnet will use the central Members Default Fund, to which all clearing members contribute, to recover losses

See Section 1.3 of your Study Text

20. **A** The concept of maintenance margin is a system where variation margin payments are taken from initial margin until a floor level is reached whereupon the member will be required to replenish his account to the original initial margin level. This system is not operated by LCH.Clearnet in the UK

See Section 2.1.2 of your Study Text

21. **A** The margin requirements relate to the overall risk of a member defaulting, and may be reduced if the member has offsetting positions

See Section 2.8 of your Study Text

22. **B**   Margin will need to be paid on any option purchased where the premium has not been settled up front. In practice, this means everything except equity and equity index options

See Section 2.8 of your Study Text

23. **B**   NYSE Liffe have price limits on the Japanese Government Bond (JGB) future. The LME occasionally introduces price limits

See Section 2.2.1 of your Study Text

24. **A**   A difficult choice. Technically speaking, clearing and settlement are two different parts of the process. Whereas B describes settlement, A is closer to clearing, which describes the parts of the process leading up to the final settlement

See Section 1 of your Study Text

25. **A**   Japanese, Swiss and Norwegian bonds are not acceptable. German equities are not acceptable. **Note**: UK, US or other equities are now NOT allowable as collateral

See Section 3.1 of your Study Text

26. **B**   Initial margin is a 'good faith' deposit that is returned when a position is closed out

See Section 2.1.1 of your Study Text

27. **B**   Premium is received and initial margin is due as this is a short option position. All payments are due by 09:00 T + 1 through the PPS. We must assume they are equity or index options since all answers imply premiums are paid upfront

See Section 2.5.1 of your Study Text

28. **B**   Position limits prevent any single member from gaining a dominant position in a contract and thereby being able to distort the market. Price limits are designed to reduce volatility

See Section 2.2 of your Study Text

29. **D**   FSA rules require brokers to charge at least the same margin to their clients as they must pay to the clearing house. A client has five business days leeway to pay the margin to their broker after which the broker is required to close out the client's position. Closing out the position would result in a limited loss being crystalised – it is while a short futures position is open that the loss is potentially unlimited

See Section 3.2 of your Study Text

30. **C**   The firm may pay margin monies out of their own money to cover both their own losses on proprietary trades and the losses of clients. The FSA is only concerned that if the firm is paying its own money to cover the positions of private customers then it does not do it for more than five business days without prior written consent

See Section 3.2 of your Study Text

31. D   All brokers are obliged to provide best execution

See Section 1.6 of your Study Text

32. **C**   Counterparty risk is present in an OTC trade where there is a risk of non-payment by the counterparty

See Section 2.9 of your Study Text

33.   **D**   It is only when a trade has been matched via an exchange's matching system that LCH.Clearnet will novate the trade

See Section 6.2 of your Study Text

34.   **C**   If there is a dramatic movement in the price of the contract then LCH.Clearnet might find itself exposed to losses over and above the initial margin that it is holding against each trading party. Intra day margin must be paid same day else contracts are closed out

See Section 2.1.1 of your Study Text

35.   **B**   Individual clearing members can only clear trades for themselves and their own clients

See Section 1.1 of your Study Text

36.   **C**   Both types of spread will benefit from reduced margins but since intra market spreads are in the same contract the off-setting feature will be greater

See Section 2.6.3 of your Study Text

37.   **A**   Clearing is actually very difficult to define but this is the best description given the available options

See Section 1 of your Study Text

6. Trading, Hedging and Investment Strategies

Questions

1. **A long hedge is**

    A   A stop order

    B   Selling short

    C   Buying futures

    D   None of the above

2. **A farmer wishing to lock into a fixed sales price for his future wheat harvest would**

    A   Buy a future

    B   Buy a call

    C   Sell a future

    D   Buy a put

3. **Which of the following is the best definition of hedging?**

    A   Speculative trading in derivatives

    B   Writing put options to protect against a fall in an underlying asset held

    C   Agreeing to repurchase bonds sold at a later date

    D   A guard against adverse price or interest rate changes

4. **A farmer looking to secure a minimum sale price for his wheat harvest, but to still leave potential for further profit, would**

    A   Buy a call

    B   Buy a put

    C   Buy a future

    D   Sell a future

5. **An investor holds 10,000 ABC plc shares. Which of the following option trades would best be used to hedge the downside but retain the upside?**

    A   Buy 100 puts

    B   Sell 100 calls

    C   Buy 10 puts

    D   Sell 10 puts

6. **An investor has bought a security which he now believes is going to fall in price. Which two of the following would be appropriate trades?**

       I   Long call

       II   Short call

       III   Long put

       IV   Short put

  A I and II

  B I and III

  C II and IV

  D II and III

7. **If a fund manager has a portfolio of £10m worth of shares representative of the FTSE-100 index and wishes to hedge that position by buying put options, how many should be bought if the index level is 5200 and the options have a strike price of 5250?**

  A 192

  B 190

  C 1,923

  D 1,905

8. **Which of the following trades would you recommend to a risk-averse investor anticipating a rise in market volatility?**

  A Long straddle

  B Short strangle

  C Horizontal spread

  D Long call

9. **If an investor sold one June 100 call for 22 and bought one September 100 call for 30 with the underlying at 100, what is his long-term market view?**

  A Neutral

  B Volatile

  C Bullish

  D Bearish

10. **If an investor bought one June 100 call for 21 and sold one June 100 put at 18, what would be his market view?**

  A Neutral

  B Volatile

  C Bullish

  D Bearish

11. **If an investor bought one June 100 call at 22 and bought one June 100 put at 18, his market view would be?**

    A   Neutral

    B   Volatile

    C   Bullish

    D   Bearish

12. **A futures trader expects the differential between near and forward to narrow. The market is currently in contango. What spread or trade should he execute?**

    A   Buy the spread

    B   Sell the spread

    C   Buy near, buy forward

    D   Sell near, sell forward

13. **Which of the following does not present arbitrage possibilities?**

    A   The price of buying the future differs to creating a synthetic long with options

    B   Buying the futures spread varies to the price of entering into the individual positions

    C   Buying and selling options with different expiries whilst anticipating increasing volatility

    D   An increase in the value of shares within an index and a simultaneous fall in the index future

14. **You believe a stock index is about to become more volatile. You buy a put for January at 2400 for 75 and buy a call for January at 2400 for 55 when the underlying is at 2380. In order that you make a profit at expiry, beyond which prices must the index lie?**

    A   2345-2455

    B   2270-2530

    C   2325-2475

    D   2318-2482

15. **Which of the following NYSE Liffe equity option trades would require margin?**

    I   A bull call spread

    II   A bull put spread

    III   A bear call spread

    IV   A bear put spread

    A   I only

    B   II only

    C   I and IV

    D   II and III

16. **How would you create a synthetic long?**

A Buy a call and buy a put

B Buy a call and sell a put

C Sell a call and sell a put

D Sell a call and buy a put

---

17. **If you were to buy a future and buy a put option on the same future, you would create**

A Synthetic long call

B Synthetic short call

C Synthetic long put

D Synthetic short put

---

18. **If you were to buy a FTSE 100 4500 put and to also buy a FTSE 100 4500 call with both options having the same expiry, what trade has been created?**

A Long strangle

B Synthetic long

C Long straddle

D Covered call

---

19. **An investor buys a September 88 T-bond put and sells a September 86 T-bond put. This is an example of**

A Bear put spread

B Bull put spread

C Synthetic long put

D Diagonal put spread

---

20. **The simultaneous purchase of July futures and the sale of September futures on Bunds is an**

A Intermarket spread

B Intramarket spread

C Interdelivery spread

D Intradelivery spread

---

21. **Which of the following gives a synthetic long call?**

A Long the underlying, short the put

B Long the underlying, long the put

C Short the underlying, short the put

D Long the underlying, long the call

22. **Which two of the following are not spread trades?**

     I   Buy June 330 put, sell June 300 put
     II   Buy June 300 call, sell Sept 330 call
     III   Buy June 330 call, buy Sept 390 call
     IV   Buy June 300 call, sell June 300 put

   A   I and II
   B   II and III
   C   II and IV
   D   III and IV

23. **All of the following are types of spread, except**

   A   Vertical bull
   B   Horizontal
   C   Lateral
   D   Diagonal

24. **Which of the following is the best description of a spread order?**

   A   A large order to be executed in several small trades
   B   The bid always being quoted before the offer
   C   Buy a future one month, sell a future another month
   D   Execute several trades at the same time

25. **A bear spread is constructed by which two of the following?**

     I   Selling a call and buying a call with a higher strike price
     II   Buying a call and selling a call with a higher strike price
     III   Selling a put and buying a put with a higher strike price
     IV   Buying a put and selling a put with a higher strike price

   A   I and IV
   B   II and III
   C   I and III
   D   II and IV

26. **If you were to purchase a low-strike put and sell a high-strike put for the same expiry date on the same underlying asset, which of the following would best describe your trade?**

   A   Bull spread
   B   Bear spread
   C   Intramarket spread
   D   Intermarket spread

27. **Your client has entered into a bear spread. Which of the following would be your advice on margin requirements?**

   A   No margin is required as it is a debit spread

   B   SPAN will not need to margin spreads

   C   The two option trades will cancel out to leave no margin

   D   A reduced form of margin will be payable due to capped profits and losses

28. **Which two of the following trades would be classified as spreads?**

   I   Long 300 August Tesco call and short 350 December Tesco call

   II   Short September gilt future and long December gilt future

   III   Short 3800 FTSE 100 March call and long 3800 FTSE 100 March put

   IV   Short 100 October Vodafone call and short 120 October Vodafone put

   A   I and II

   B   II and IV

   C   II and III

   D   I and IV

29. **An investor buys a call on the Euribor future. The investor also buys a put on the Euribor future at the same strike price. The investor has**

   A   A short straddle

   B   A long straddle

   C   A long strangle

   D   A short strangle

30. **What is the best definition of an equity hedge?**

   A   Having a short or long position in the underlying equity offset by a long or short futures trade

   B   Trading derivatives around an underlying long equity position

   C   Using a bond portfolio to reduce the risk of an equity portfolio

   D   Using put call parity to construct a synthetic long position

31. **How many bond futures would be required to hedge a holding of £150m of the cheapest-to-deliver gilt? The future has a nominal value of £100,000 and the cheapest-to-deliver price factor is 1.151617**

   A   1,303 contracts

   B   1,500 contracts

   C   1,727 contracts

   D   1,839 contracts

32. **Five gilt futures are sold at 100.10. The EDSP is £103.10 for £100 nominal. The future is £100,000 nominal per contract. What is the invoice amount for the cheapest-to-deliver with a price factor of 1.212121 disregarding accrued interest?**

   A   £85,058

   B   £124,970

   C   £425,288

   D   £624,848

33. **The June FTSE future is trading at 6095 with a tick value of £5 per half index point. How many futures contracts should a fund manager with £4.15m of FTSE 100 equities trade?**

   A   34

   B   68

   C   102

   D   136

34. **If the cheapest-to-deliver gilt against the UK gilt futures contract has a coupon of 5% and the notional coupon of the future is 6%, a hedge of a holding of the CTD would involve**

   A   Buying futures equivalent to the face value of the bondholding

   B   Selling futures equivalent to the face value of the bondholding

   C   Selling futures equivalent to more than the face value of the bondholding

   D   Selling futures equivalent to less than the face value of the bondholding

35. **A UK borrower seeking to fix his costs would**

   A   Buy three-month sterling futures

   B   Sell three-month sterling futures

   C   Buy three-month sterling calls

   D   Buy three-month sterling puts

36. **You own a portfolio of bonds and you are concerned that interest rates may rise in the near future. Which of the following strategies could you employ to protect the value of your portfolio?**

   A   Sell a bond put option

   B   Buy a bond with high volatility and sell a lower volatility bond

   C   Sell long bond futures

   D   Buy a bond call option

37.   **An investor buys 13 FTSE futures at 6105 on Day 1. At the end of Day 1, the settlement price is 6098. At the end of Day 2, the settlement price is 6103. If an index point is £10, what is the variation margin on Day 2?**

A   £260 debit

B   £50 credit

C   £650 credit

D   £20 debit

38.   **What is the maximum risk if you buy a futures contract?**

A   Unlimited

B   Limited to the premium paid

C   Limited to the initial margin

D   Limited to the price paid

39.   **The minimum price movement on a futures contract is known as a**

A   Spread

B   Tick

C   Pip

D   Point

40.   **A gilt trader buys five contracts at 103.10, and subsequently closes his position at 104.17. The tick size is 0.01 and the tick value £10. What is his profit?**

A   £1,070

B   £5,350

C   £609.38

D   £452.31

41.   **A speculator believes that the price of coffee will go up and buys two coffee futures contracts at $810. Two weeks later, the market has moved up and the trader closes out his position at $840. Commission is a round turn $20 per contract. What is his profit/loss? (1 contract = 5 tonnes)**

A $300 loss

B $30 profit

C $300 profit

D $260 profit

42.   **The maximum risk from selling a futures contract is**

A   Limited to the value of the future

B   Unlimited

C   Limited to the initial margin deposit

D   Limited as the market cannot fall below zero

43. **An investor goes long of five Bund futures at 108.98 and subsequently sells them at 109.98. If the futures contract size is €100,000 what percentage return is made on an initial margin of €500 per contract?**

   A   50%

   B   75%

   C   100%

   D   200%

44. **All of the following are possible descriptions of the maximum loss from a long future, except**

   A   Large but limited

   B   Almost unlimited

   C   Price of the future

   D   Unlimited

45. **Which of the following is a speculative trade?**

   A   An investor who anticipates a fall in the market buying a put option

   B   An investor who anticipates a rise in the market buying a call option

   C   An investor buying a call option and selling a put option with the same strike and expiry date

   D   An investor buying a call option and buying a put option with the same strike and expiry date

46. **In February, the NYSE Liffe interest rate contracts for March-September stood at +25 ticks. If an intramarket spreader buys the spread, which two of the following statements are true in respect of his actions?**

   I   The March contract is bought and the September contract is sold

   II   The September contract is bought and the March contract is sold

   III He believes that the yield curve will steepen

   IV   He believes that the yield curve will flatten

   A   I and III

   B   II and III

   C   I and IV

   D   II and IV

47. **An investor is short eight futures and short four ATM put options in the same underlying asset. What is his net position in terms of future?**

   A   Short 4 futures

   B   Short 6 futures

   C   Short 10 futures

   D   Short 12 futures

48.   What does it mean to be short in the physical commodity?

A   To not have the commodity now but to have a need to buy it in the future

B   To have the underlying physical commodity and to also hold a short position in the related futures contract

C   To have the physical commodity now but to be committed to selling it

D   To not have the physical commodity but to have a short futures position on the commodity

49.   What type of trade is most commonly used in anticipation of key announcements by the issuer of a security?

A   Horizontal spread

B   Covered call

C   Bull vertical spread

D   Bear vertical spread

50.   If an investor is long a 700 Tesco put, how could he create a bear vertical spread?

A   Long 600 Tesco put

B   Short 600 Tesco put

C   Long 800 Tesco put

D   Short 800 Tesco put

51.   What is the major use of sythetics?

A   Speculation

B   Arbitrage

C   To take advantage of changes in liquidity

D   Basis trades

Answers

1. **C** The hedge takes its name from the trade conducted on the derivatives market to hedge the underlying position

   See Section 3.9 of your Study Text

2. **C** The farmer has a long position in the underlying wheat, since he would lose out if the price falls. To hedge this position he would sell a future (profit if price falls). The name of the hedge is given by the future trade and therefore, this would be a short hedge. The long put would not fix the price, but rather provide a floor below which the price at which the farmer can sell would not fall. However, with a long put, the farmer has retained the upside

   See Section 3.8 of your Study Text

3. **D** A hedger is looking to protect himself from adverse movements in the market and can use derivatives to achieve this goal

   See Sections 3.8 and 3.9 of your Study Text

4. **B** The put ensures the minimum price, but does not limit profits (as would be the case with a short future)

   See Section 3.1 of your Study Text

5. **C** If the investor is long shares then he should buy put options. These will allow him to sell the shares at the strike price and can be exercised to prevent losses if the market falls. Each put option is the right to sell 1,000 shares. Hence, ten put option contracts should be purchased

   See Section 3.1 of your Study Text

6. **D** If the asset is expected to fall in price, the investor will make a profit with bearish trades such as the short call and the long put

   See Section 3 of your Study Text

7. **B** With options, use the strike price to calculate the hedge, rather than the index level.

   Please note that you do use the value of the index with a delta hedge (see Section 5.1 for more details)

   See Section 5.3 of your Study Text

8. **A** You can only lose the premiums when you buy the call and the put to construct the long straddle. It is a volatility trade so will benefit if either the price moves up (long call wins) or down (long put wins)

   See Sections 3.7 of your Study Text

9. **B** Horizontal spreads exploit volatility. Vertical spreads exploit bullish/bearish markets

   See Section 3.11 of your Study Text

10. **C** A synthetic long. Thus exploiting a bullish market

    See Section 3.2 of your Study Text

11. **B** A long strangle exploits volatility

See Section 3.7.4 of your Study Text

12. **A** Buy the near and sell the far. The trade takes its name from what you do with the near-dated. In a contango market the far-dated future is trading at a higher price than the near-dated. As this gap is expected to close the far-dated will fall in value relative to the near-dated, so sell the far-dated

See Section 2.1 of your Study Text

13. **C** Arbitrage possibilities exist where two related instruments are mispriced relative to each other and are characterised by the opportunity for risk-free profits. Answer C is a horizontal option spread, which is not a risk-free arbitrage trade

See Section 3.11 of your Study Text

14. **B** Overall, you have bought a put option and a call option with the same strike and same expiry. Hence, the overall position is a 'long straddle'. The long straddle is a volatility trade that will be profitable if the market falls by the sum of both premiums below the strike, or rises by the sum of both premiums above the strike

Lower breakeven point: Strike – Sum of both premiums

$$2400 - (75 + 55) = 2270$$

Upper breakeven point: Strike + Sum of both premiums

$$2400 + (75 + 55) = 2530$$

NB: The premiums in this question are quoted in points, not pence

See Section 3.7.2 of your Study Text

15. **D** Only spreads which are dealt for a credit require margin

See Section 3.3 of your Study Text

16. **B** The synthetic long is created by buying a call and selling a put. Selling a call and buying a put creates the synthetic short. The relationship between the price of the call and the put and the futures price is measured by the put/call parity theorem

See Section 3.2 of your Study Text

17. **A** The long put protects you on the downside, but allows you the upside from the long future. Hence, we have created a synthetic long call

See Section 3.2 of your Study Text

18. **C** Buying a call and a put with the same strike and expiry creates a long straddle

See Section 3.7.2 of your Study Text

19. **A** The options are the same type, so it is a spread. You bought the high strike and sold the low strike, so it is a bear spread

See Section 3.3 of your Study Text

20. **B** 'Intra' because it is within the same Bunds market. 'Inter' would be a purchase and sale between two different but related markets

See Section 2.1 of your Study Text

21. **B** Going long the underlying and then buying a put creates a synthetic long call position

See Section 3.2 of your Study Text

22. **D** A spread trade is one that involves the buying and selling of options of the same type. For example, buying a call and selling a call with a different strike (vertical), or buying a put and selling a put with a different expiry (horizontal). Remember that buying or selling a call and a put is a combination trade

See Section 3.11 of your Study Text

23. **C** Vertical spreads have the same expiry but different strikes, horizontal spreads have the same strike but different expiry dates and diagonal spreads have different strikes and different expiry dates. Laterals are not spreads

See Section 3.11 of your Study Text

24. **C** Answer B is describing the spread – the difference between the bid price and the offer price. Buying a future in one month and selling a future another month, e.g. buying the December FTSE 100 index future and selling the March FTSE 100 index future is called buying the spread and is an example of an intramarket spread order

See Section 2.1 of your Study Text

25. **C** For a bear spread buy the high strike and sell the low strike, with either both calls or both puts

See Section 3.3 of your Study Text

26. **A** This a vertical spread, since they both have the same expiry but different strike prices. Buying the low-strike option and selling the high-strike is a bull spread

See Section 3.3 of your Study Text

27. **D** A bear spread could be constructed with calls or puts and be a debit or a credit spread. There is a reduced form of margining because of the restricted profit and loss outcomes in a spread

See Section 3.3 of your Study Text

28. **A** The short call with the long put would be a synthetic short future. The short call with the short put would be a short strangle. Neither of these are spread trades

See Sections 2.1, 2.2 and 3.11 of your Study Text

29. **B** Buying a put and a call with the same strike and expiry creates a long straddle. Hence, the investor believes that volatility will be higher than is implied by current option premiums

See Section 3.7.2 of your Study Text

30. **A** This is the best available answer as the underlying equity position need not be long

See Sections 3.8 and 3.9 of your Study Text

31. **C** The number of futures required to hedge the cheapest-to-deliver (CTD) holding is as follows

$$\text{Number of futures} = \frac{\text{CTD holding}}{\text{NV of gilt future}} \times \text{Pricing factor}$$

$$= \frac{£150,000,000}{£100,000} \times 1.151617$$

$$= 1,727 \text{ contracts}$$

See Section 4.1.3 of your Study Text

32. **D** Invoice amount $= (\text{EDSP} \times \text{Scaling factor}) \times \text{No. of contracts} \times \text{Price factor}$

$$= £103.10 \times \frac{£100,000 \text{ NV}}{£100 \text{ NV}} \times 5 \times 1.212121$$

$$= £103.10 \times 1,000 \times 5 \times 1.212121$$

$$= £624,848.38$$

The most appropriate answer is £624,848

See Section 4.1.1 of your Study Text

33. **B** The number of futures required to hedge the existing portfolio in the short term would be

$$\text{No. of futures required} = \frac{\text{Value of existing portfolio}}{\text{FTSE future index value} \times £10 \text{ per point}}$$

$$= \frac{£4.15m}{6095 \times £10 \text{ per point}}$$

$$= 68 \text{ futures contracts}$$

Please note that if the title value is £5 per half index point, this equates to £10 per full index point. Furthermore, we are not given a value for beta so we assume that it is 1

See Section 4.3 of your Study Text

34. **D** To hedge a holding of the CTD, selling futures would be required. The number of futures required to hedge is given by the formula

$$\text{No. of futures} = \frac{\text{Holding of CTD}}{\text{NV of gilt future}} \times \text{Price factor of CTD}$$

If the CTD coupon (5%) is less than the coupon (6%) of the notional gilt future, then the price factor would be less than 1. Therefore, the number of contracts would be less than the simple division of the nominal value by the futures face value

See Section 4.1.3 of your Study Text

35. **B** A borrower is concerned about interest rates rising. Therefore, if interest rates were to rise, the three-month short sterling (STIR) future would fall in value (as it is priced at 100 – interest rate). Therefore, the borrower would sell three-month short sterling futures. This future would fix the rate or lock in the price, whereas the put option, although bearish, would simply establish a maximum cost

See Section 4.2 of your Study Text

36.   **C**   To hedge a holding of the underlying asset, you need to either short the future or go long the put. Note that the expression 'long' in the instruction to sell the **long** bond future refers to the long-dated nature of the bond (i.e. a bond with ten years to maturity) and so as the future is being sold, it will result in a short future on that long-dated bond

See Section 3.8 of your Study Text

37.   **C**   Profit/loss = Ticks moved × Tick value × No. of contracts

= (6103 − 6098) × £10 × 13 = £650 credit/profit

See Section 1.3 of your Study Text

38.   **D**   The price cannot fall below zero, therefore the maximum loss is the contract price

See Section 1.2 of your Study Text

39.   **B**   Tick is the name given to the minimum permitted price movement on a futures contract. For example, if the tick on a wheat future is 5p per tonne, this would mean that the price of wheat can move in multiples of 5p only. Pip is sometimes used for the FX forward premium or discount price movements

See Section 1.3 of your Study Text

40.   **B**   Profit = Number of ticks price has moved × Tick value × Number of contracts

$$= \frac{(104.17 - 103.10)}{0.01} \times £10 \times \text{Five contracts}$$

= 107 ticks × £10 × Five contracts

∴ Profit = £5,350

See Section 1.3 of your Study Text

41.   **D**   The term 'round turn' incorporates the cost of both buying and selling

Profit/Loss   = Ticks × Tick value × No. of contracts

= 30 × ($1 × 5) × 2

= $300

Less Commission = $300 − (2 × $20)

= $260

See Section 1.3 of your Study Text

42.   **B**   The maximum risk is the maximum loss, which is unlimited for short futures positions

See Section 1.4 of your Study Text

43.   **D** $(109.98 - 108.98) \times \dfrac{€100,000}{100} = €1,000$ profit

Return $= \dfrac{€1,000}{€500} \times 100 = 200\%$

See Section 1.3 of your Study Text

44. **D** A long future makes losses if the price falls. The worst case scenario is if the price falls to zero. This is therefore not unlimited, but could potentially be described as large but limited, almost unlimited or the price of the future

See Section 1.2 of your Study Text

45. **C** C is a synthetic long. In fact, all of the trades given are speculative, but the risk of A, B and D are limited to option premiums, whereas the risk of the synthetic long is large but limited (almost unlimited). Hence, C is the most speculative trade, which we assume, therefore, makes it the best available answer

See Section 3.2 of your Study Text

46. **A** Buying the spread means buy the near-dated contract (March) and sell the far-dated contract (September). For a profit, you need the March future to rise (i.e. short-term interest rates to fall) and the September future to fall (i.e. longer term rates to rise). This will make the yield curve steeper

See Section 2.1 of your Study Text

47. **B** A future has a delta of 1 and an at-the-money option has a delta of 0.5. Since bullish positions have positive delta and bearish positions have negative delta, the overall position is

$(8 \times -1) + (4 \times 0.5) = -6$

This is equivalent to being short six futures

See Section 5.1 of your Study Text

48. **A** Note that the distractors were referring to a basis trade and to being short in the futures market (not the physical market as asked)

See Section 3.9 of your Study Text

49. **A** The horizontal spread is a volatility trade that can take advantage of any short term price moves that result from the new information

See Section 3.11 of your Study Text

50. **B** For a bear spread, we buy the high strike and sell the low strike. Therefore we need to simultaneously sell the 600 put. Bear spreads can of course be created with two calls or two puts, both giving limited profit if the market drops, and limited gains if the market rises

See Section 3.11 of your Study Text

51. **B** Synthetics allow users to take advantage of arbitrage opportunities from mispriced investments

See Section 3.2 of your Study Text

7. Special Regulatory Requirements

Questions

1. **CFTC stands for**

    A   The Commission for Futures Trading in Commodities

    B   The Commission Firms Trading Council

    C   The Commodities and Financial Trade Council

    D   The Commodity Futures Trading Commission

2. **Members of the CFTC are authorised by which of the following bodies?**

    A   SEC

    B   FIA

    C   NFA

    D   MFA

3. **The responsibility for regulating US futures trading lies with**

    A   SEC

    B   Congress

    C   CFTC

    D   NFA

4. **Non-US firms wishing to trade directly on US exchanges for US citizens may do so, if they**

    A   Apply for Part 30 exemption

    B   Abide by Part 30

    C   Register with the NFA

    D   Advise the FSA

5. **Which one of the following would not be regulated by the SEC?**

    A   Trades in S&P options

    B   Trades on CBOE

    C   Trades on CBOT

    D   Trades in on-exchange currency derivatives

6. **Who is the main regulator of the futures markets in the US?**

    A   SEC

    B   NFA

    C   CFTC

    D   FSA

7. **IAS 19 states that embedded derivatives must be valued in which of the following ways?**

   A Embedded derivatives need not be valued by institutions

   B Embedded value need only be valued when separated from their instruments

   C Embedded derivatives must be valued with their host instruments

   D Embedded derivatives need only be valued at exercise

8. **What is the best description of the CFTC Part 30 exemption?**

   A It allows resident US investors to trade on US exchanges

   B It allows resident US investors to trade on non US exchanges

   C It allows non resident US investors to trade on US exchanges

   D It allows non resident US investors to trade on non US exchanges

9. **An advisor comes to realise that a client is trading futures for investment rather than commercial reasons. When will the provisions of MiFID apply?**

   A Immediately

   B No later than the next business day

   C In five business days

   D In seven calendar days

10. **A broker has two clients. One is classed as a professional client, the other as a retail client. Which of the following is false?**

   A The professional client may require less disclosure of risks

   B The retail client's trades take precedence over the professional client's trades

   C The full scope of MiFID applies to the client relationship of both clients

   D Retail customers are assumed to be the least sophisticated of client types

11. **What is a benefit of principles based regulation?**

   A Less intervention

   B Increased flexibility

   C Cheaper regulation

   D None of the above

12. **If a client is dealing in commodity derivatives for commercial reasons, what can they opt out of?**

   A Sarbanes-Oxley

   B CFTC part 30

   C MiFID

   D None of the above

13.   **What is the main requirement imposed by IAS 39?**

A   All cash positions should be hedged

B   All listed companies should produce a cash flow statement

C   All derivatives should be shown on the balance sheet at fair value

D   All financial institutions should have sufficient capital to manage their risks

14.   **Which of the following is the best description of the status of the NFA?**

A   A self-regulated organisation overseen by the CFTC

B   A self-regulated organisation overseen by the SEC

C   An organisation regulated by the CFTC

D   An organisation regulated by the SEC

Answers

1. **D** The CFTC is an abbreviation for the Commodity Futures Trading Commission. The CFTC regulates all on-exchange derivatives trading, with the exception of those areas covered by the SEC

    See Section 2.3 of your Study Text

2. **C** The National Futures Association (NFA) acts as a self-regulatory organisation for futures firms using delegated powers from The Commodity Futures Trading Commission (CFTC). Therefore, derivative firms in the US are authorised by the NFA, whereas it is the SEC who authorise securities firms

    See Section 2.2 of your Study Text

3. **C** The best available answer as most futures are regulated by the Commodity Futures Trading Commission (CFTC). The SEC only regulates limited financial derivatives such as stock options and stock index options

    See Section 2.2 of your Study Text

4. **C** Part 30 exemption is only required when trading for US citizens on non-US exchanges. A non-US firm can trade on US exchanges for US citizens as long as they register with the National Futures Association (NFA) or deal through a suitable NFA member

    See Section 2.4 of your Study Text

5. **C** The Chicago Board of Trade (CBOT) is regulated by the CFTC. As a memory technique for the exam, try using the following mnemonic: The SEC regulates S for **S**ecurities (i.e. the NYSE), E for **E**quity index derivatives (and hence the Chicago Board **O**f **E**xchange where you trade **O**ptions on **E**quities) and C for **C**urrency derivatives on exchange. The **CFTC** regulates the remaining **CME** products such as **C**ommodities and **T**-bond futures on the CBOT

    See Section 2.3 of your Study Text

6. **C** The CFTC unlike the SEC only regulate derivatives and oversee the National Futures Association

    See Section 2.2 of your Study Text

7. **C** Embedded derivatives must be marked to market in exactly the same way as other derivatives

    See Section 3 of your Study Text

8. **B** The CFTC part 30 exemption protects US resident citizens when trading outside to US. Firms outside the US may only do business with US resident citizens if they have the part 30 exemption which provides the US customers with a basic level of protection even when trading offshore (e.g. the right to sue in the US courts, seek arbitration from the US regulator and get the US version of the warrant and derivative risk warning – the CFTC risk disclosure)

    See Section 2.4.1 of your Study Text

9. **A** MiFID will apply immediately

    See Section1 of your Study Text

10. **B** One client's trades should not take automatic precedence over another

See Section 2.2 of your Study Text

11. **B** The increased flexibility is particularly important in today's ever changing markets

See Section 2.1 of your Study Text

12. **C** MiFID rules can be applied to contracts undertaken for commercial purposes, but they do not have to be

See Section 2 of your Study Text

13. **C** This is not strictly true since derivatives used as a hedge do not have to be shown at fair value. However, this is the best answer available

See Section 4 of your Study Text

14. **A** The examiner often asks questions about regulation in the US markets

See Section 3.3 of your Study Text

Practice
Examinations

Contents

Practice Examination 1

75 Questions in 1 hour 30 minutes

1. An investor buys a call option with a strike of 100 for a premium of 6. He also sells the underlying asset for 101. Calculate the maximum profit of this strategy

    A 94

    B 95

    C 96

    D 97

2. In terms of trading, gearing is best described as

    A Variation margin

    B Option premium in relation to the price of the underlying asset

    C The credit line available to a speculator

    D A prime brokerage account

3. If an investor had an expectation that the Eurozone yield curve would rotate and flatten at the longer end, what spread trade would make sense?

    A Buy the Euribor future and sell the Bund future

    B Sell the Euribor future and sell the Bund future

    C Buy the Bund future and sell the Euribor future

    D Buy the Euribor future and sell the Eurodollar future

4. Which two of the following factors would cause an increase in option premiums if the factor were to increase?

    I   Time to expiry

    II   Volatility

    III Interest rates

    IV Price of the underlying

    A I and II

    B II and III

    C III and IV

    D I and IV

5. **Which of the following is a contango market?**

    A   The synthetic is cheaper than the underlying

    B   The synthetic is more expensive than the underlying

    C   Near-dated prices are lower than far-dated prices

    D   Far-dated prices are lower than near-dated prices

6. **Which two of the following are true of an in-the-money call option?**

    I   The option will have intrinsic value

    II   The strike price will exceed the price of the underlying

    III   The strike price will be lower than the price of the underlying

    IV   The option will have no intrinsic value

    A   I and III

    B   II and IV

    C   I and II

    D   III and IV

7. **If the change in an option premium is the same as a change in the underlying, which of the following would be the option's delta?**

    A   0.5

    B   1.0

    C   0.1

    D   3.0

8. **An investor buys a long gilt call with a strike price of 97.00 for a premium of 30 basis points. The investor also sells a put option on the long gilt at the same strike for 20 basis points. Which of the following reflects the investor's position?**

    A   A synthetic long future at 96.90

    B   A synthetic short future at 96.90

    C   A synthetic long future at 97.10

    D   A synthetic short future at 97.10

9. **A depositor who wanted to protect against an adverse move in interest rates would**

    A   Buy a collar

    B   Sell a floor

    C   Sell a collar

    D   Sell a cap

10. **An investor wishes to place an order to sell when the price drops to 97, although they are willing to sell at prices higher than that. Which of the following would be the best order?**

A Stop order

B MIT order

C Stop limit order

D Market order

11. **Why would an investor buy a horizontal call spread?**

A In anticipation of a fall in volatility

B In anticipation of a rise in price

C In anticipation of a rise in volatility

D In anticipation of a rise in price

12. **Which of the following best describes a cross trade?**

A Where one firm handles both the buy and sell side of a trade

B Where a firm executes a large number of orders with the same counterparty

C A trade executed across the floor of an exchange

D Simultaneous trades in the cash and futures markets

13. **The process by which LCH.Clearnet becomes a counterparty to all trades is known as**

A Clearing

B Settlement

C Nomination

D Novation

14. **Which of following is a speculative trade?**

A An investor who anticipates a fall in the market buying a put option

B An investor who anticipates a rise in the market buying a call option

C An investor buying a call option and selling a put option with the same strike and expiry date

D An investor buying a call option and buying a put option with the same strike and expiry date

15. **Which two of the following are true with regard to an option on a future traded on NYSE Liffe?**

I   The premium is paid upfront

II   Long positions are margined

III   The premium is paid on close

IV   Only short positions are margined

A I and II

B II and III

C III and IV

D I and IV

16. **An investor holding an FRN would protect against falling interest rates by entering the following?**

    A   Asset swap

    B   Pay fixed swap

    C   Receive fixed swap

    D   Roller coaster swap

17. **An investor is long the underlying asset and owns a put option on the same asset. Which of the following strategies would eliminate the market risk of this position using put-call parity theory?**

    A   Short underlying and short put

    B   Short call and long underlying

    C   Synthetic long call

    D   Synthetic long put

18. **An increase in the delta of an equity call option is most likely to result in**

    A   An increase in variation margin for the long position

    B   An increase in variation margin for the short position

    C   A decrease in variation margin for the long position

    D   A decrease in variation margin for the short position

19. **Which of the following swaps would not have a notional principal which varies over the life of the agreement?**

    A   Amortising

    B   Arrears

    C   Accreting

    D   Rollercoaster

20. **Which of the following is not a type of currency swap?**

    A   Floating – floating currency swap

    B   Fixed – fixed currency swap

    C   Cross currency swap

    D   Cross currency basis swap

21.   **An investor is short the Long Gilt future. Which two of the following are true?**

  I   The investor may believe interest rates will rise

  II   The investor must believe that bond prices will rise

  III   The contract may be closed out by buying the STIR future

  IV   If left open, the investor will have to physically deliver

A   I and II

B   III and IV

C   II and III

D   I and IV

22.   **Which of the following will be true of the cheapest-to-deliver gilt?**

A   It will produce the lowest fair value using actual repo rates

B   It will have the highest actual repo rate

C   It will have the highest implied repo rate

D   It will be the cheapest gilt

23.   **If an investor holding a basket of equities is concerned about falling prices, which type of swap would be consider as a hedging instrument?**

A   Volatility swap

B   Total return swap

C   Accreting swap

D   Commodity swap

24.   **Which of the following is not a credit event?**

A   Bankruptcy

B   Repudiation

C   Debt restructuring

D   Maturity

25.   **The US regulations contained in CFTC Part 30 (foreign futures and options) relate to which of the following?**

A   A US investor wishing to trade on a US exchange

B   A US investor wishing to trade on NYSE Liffe

C   A US affiliate of the UK company wishing to trade on NYSE Liffe

D   A UK investor currently residing in the US wishing to trade on NYSE Liffe

26. **Which two of the following options are out-of-the-money?**

    I   April 150 call with a premium of 10 when the underlying is trading at 155

    II   May 220 put with a premium of 5 when the underlying is trading at 220

    III   June 180 call with a premium of 12 when the underlying is trading at 170

    IV   May 550 put with a premium of 18 when the underlying is trading at 575

    A   III and IV

    B   I and II

    C   II and III

    D   II and IV

27. **Which of the following is a type of credit derivative?**

    A   Credit default swap

    B   Default

    C   Bankruptcy

    D   Moratorium

28. **Which of the following would be the main reason why an investor may wish to trade an exchange traded derivative?**

    A   They will pay lower margin

    B   They will pay lower fees

    C   The product will offer greater flexibility

    D   There will be lower credit default risk

29. **How can a credit default swap be settled?**

    A   Cash only

    B   Cash or physically

    C   Physically only

    D   Neither in cash or physically

30. **Which of the following swaps would most efficiently hedge against market perception that credit conditions are deteriorating, when there has been no official credit rating downgrade?**

    A   Credit spread put option

    B   Credit spread call option

    C   Credit default swap

    D   Asset swap

31. **Which of the following is a reason for buying a call option?**

A   To enable you to have the right to sell an asset

B   To earn extra income

C   To profit from a bearish market

D   To hedge a short underlying position

32. **What should be included in the calculation of an index future's fair value?**

    I   Interest rates

    II   Margin payments

    III   Market sentiment

    IV   Brokers fees

A   I only

B   I and II

C   I and III

D   I, II, III and IV

33. **An investor is long 5 September short sterling futures and long 10 Dec short sterling futures and wants reduced margin payments. Will this be allowed?**

A   Yes as the risk is offset

B   No margin will be required for this position

C   No reduction will be allowed

D   An additional margin will be payable over the individual positions

34. **Which of the following statements is false?**

A   If short-term interest rates are less than the return on an underlying asset, a future will be at a discount to the cash price

B   All hedges will suffer if basis weakens

C   If you sell an intramarket spread, you will benefit if cost of carry increases

D   In a contango market, cost of longer dated futures would be expected to be at a premium to short-dated futures

35. **The spread on the STIR future is +25. It is now May and a trader buys the spread. What does he do and what is he expecting?**

    I   Buys the June contract and sells the September contract

    II   Sells the June contract and buys the September contract

    III   The yield curve is expected to flatten

    IV   The yield curve is expected to steepen

A   I and III

B   I and IV

C   II and III

D   II and IV

36. **Which one of the following option types will not specify the strike price in advance?**

   A   Bermudan

   B   Lookback

   C   American

   D   European

37. **The spot price of a commodity is $100 and the interest/storage costs have been calculated to be $10 per month. Which two of the following future prices could represent a potential opportunity for an arbitrageur?**

   I   Three-month future at $125

   II   Four-month future at $140

   III   Five-month future at $150

   IV   Six-month future at $155

   A   II and IV

   B   I and IV

   C   II and III

   D   I and III

38. **If you were to sell a 100 call at 7 and sell a 100 put at 5, where the underlying asset trades at 102, what prices would the underlying need to be between at expiry for a profit to arise?**

   A   95/107

   B   93/105

   C   88/112

   D   86/114

39. **Why would an investor buy a payer swaption?**

   A   To protect against credit default risk

   B   To protect against an interest rate fall

   C   To lock in a fixed rate of interest irrespective of interest rate fluctuations

   D   To protect against an interest rate rise

40. **A short futures hedge is preferable to a hedge using puts because**

   A   The short hedge retains upside potential

   B   The futures hedge is more flexible

   C   The futures hedge is cheaper

   D   The futures hedge has no basis risk

41. **Which of the following is most likely to be the motivation to do an interest rate swap?**

    A   Obtain cheaper finance

    B   Take on foreign exchange risk

    C   Hedge credit risk

    D   Reduce an equity risk position

42. **Which of the following formulae would you use to calculate the number of bond futures to sell in order to hedge a holding of £250m nominal of the cheapest to deliver (CTD)?**

    A   £250m × CTD price factor

    B $\dfrac{£250m}{\text{CTD price factor}} \times \text{Face value of future}$

    C $\dfrac{£250m}{\text{CDT price factor}} \times \text{Face value of future} + \text{Accrued interest}$

    D $\dfrac{£250m}{\text{Face value of future}} \times \text{CTD price factor}$

43. **Given the information below, what trade would be undertaken?**

    The following information reflects current market prices and rates

    FTSE 100 cash index = 5000

    FTSE 100 future price = 5080

    Risk-free rate = 4.5%

    Dividend yield = 3%

    Days to expiry = 365

    A   Buy futures and sell a FTSE 100 index tracker and put money on deposit

    B   Borrow money and buy a FTSE 100 index tracker and sell the future

    C   Do nothing, as professional arbitragers would remove any potential profit you would make

    D   Sell the FTSE 100 future as it is overpriced

44. **How do you create a synthetic index using the following derivatives on that index?**

    A   Buy a put and sell a call and hold cash

    B   Buy calls and hold cash

    C   Buy futures and hold cash

    D   Sell futures and hold cash

45. **An investor buys an FRA. Under what circumstances will they profit?**

    A   LIBOR falls

    B   LIBOR rises

    C   Interest rate volatility rises

    D   Interest rate volatility falls

46.   **Deep out-of-the-money call options**

        I   Offer the buyer a remote chance of profit

        II   Offer the writer small premiums

        III   Offer limited liquidity

        IV   Will have delta close to zero

A   I and II

B   I and III

C   II and III

D   I, II, III and IV

47.   **On which of the following trades will margin not always be payable?**

A   Buying options

B   Selling options

C   Buying futures

D   Selling futures

48.   **What is the main source for exchange price feeds?**

A   Official exchange reporting systems

B   Brokers trading reports

C   Automatic trading systems

D   Pit observers

49.   **You have a long position in a futures contract that moves adversely by 10%. The initial margin is 5% of the futures value. After the adverse move, what percentage of the futures value would you be required to pay as margin?**

A   5%

B   10%

C   20%

D   15%

50.   **Which of the following best describes a contract for a difference?**

A   A contract in which the final settlement is the final mark to market

B   A contract in which different qualities of the commodity can be delivered

C   A contract in which different quantities of a commodity can be delivered

D   An index product

51. **You are long 15 futures contracts. At which price could a stop limit order at $875 not be executed?**

A $895

B $885

C $875

D $865

52. **A hedger has sold futures contracts to protect a cash position. Throughout the life of the hedge, he will be concerned about**

A   Basis changes

B   Cash price movements

C   Futures price movements

D   Cash and futures movements

53. **At what levels will the following combined trades breakeven?**

Long 3800 call @ 78

Long 3700 put @ 85

A   3615 and 3878

B   3537 and 3963

C   3622 and 3878

D   3778 and 3722

54. **You are approached by a US domiciled citizen. You work for an FSA authorised firm. Which two of the following are you allowed or required to do?**

I   Provide segregation

II   Trade US exchange contracts

III   If your firm has not been exempted from CFTC Part 30, he may trade UK exchange contracts

IV   Trade all contracts whether US or UK

A   I and II

B   II and III

C   III and IV

D   I and IV

55. **The process by which LCH.Clearnet registers, guarantees and settles is known as**

A   Novation

B   Clearing

C   Delivery

D   Checking

56. **Which of these trades needs to be reported within five minutes?**

A   Against actuals

B   Basis

C   Block

D   Flex option

57. **Which of the following swap agreements would not have a notional principal?**

A   Accreting

B   Amortising

C   Currency

D   Rollercoaster

58. **Which one of the following is true of SPAN initial margins on options on futures?**

A   Premiums are paid upfront so no initial margin is called

B   Long positions only are margined

C   Short positions only are margined

D   Long and short positions are margined

59. **Who regulates stock index options in the US?**

A   SEC

B   CFTC

C   Federal Reserve

D   The FSA

60. **All of the following trades might properly be described as an arbitrage opportunity in equity derivatives, except**

A   If the FTSE 100 future goes down whilst the values of the constituent stock goes up

B   If you buy a call with a view to the underlying asset rising

C   If the price of the constituent legs of a spread trade differs from the market's bid/offer for the spread itself

D   If the price of the synthetic position differs from the futures price

61. **What does the term hedging mean?**

A   The opening of a position to exploit a mispricing between a synthetic position and its underlying

B   The management of risks by the use of offsetting derivative transactions

C   The securing of credit risk by depositing of collateral at a central agency

D   The closing out of a position when the underlying asset has moved in the desired direction

62. **The best description of gamma is**

    A   It is greatest for at-the-money options close to expiry

    B   the implied volatility of the change in option pricing

    C   the rate of change of delta with a change in the price of the underlying

    D   It is positive for long option positions

63. **Which of the following is the best definition of basis?**

    A   The extent to which a market is in contango

    B   The LCH.Clearnet acceptable collateral for initial margin

    C   The profit arising from a cash and carry arbitrage

    D   The result of deducting the future price from the underlying cash price

64. **If an investor is short three futures and long four deeply in-the-money puts, each of which have a delta of –1, what would be the overall net delta of this position?**

    A   Long four futures

    B   Short seven futures

    C   Short four futures

    D   Long one future

65. **An investor buys a 100 call for 7p and sells a 110 call for 3p. What is the maximum profit on this trade?**

    A   3p

    B   4p

    C   6p

    D   10p

66. **Open outcry trading has all of the following characteristics, except**

    A   Traders meet face-to-face on a trading floor

    B   Bid and offer prices are called out

    C   It is a transparent market

    D   It is a 24-hour market

67. **An investor who considers short-dated call options are trading at excessive implied volatilities would consider a**

    A   Long straddle

    B   Horizontal spread

    C   Vertical spread

    D   Short straddle

68. **Who is the main regulator of the derivatives market in the United States?**

   A   SEC

   B   CFTC

   C   NFA

   D   CME

69. **A speculator believes that the price of coffee will go up and buys two coffee futures contracts at $790 per tonne. Two weeks later, the market has moved up and the trader closes out his position at $820 per tonne. What is his profit/loss? (1 contract = 5 tonnes)**

   A $300 loss

   B $150 loss

   C $150 profit

   D $300 profit

70. **Which of the following would a depositor use for hedging purposes?**

   A   Long cap

   B   Short cap

   C   Long floor

   D   Short floor

71. **You buy ten contracts of an LME copper future for $2,710 per tonne and pay commission at $50 a round turn per contract. If you subsequently sold the contracts at $2,775 per tonne and each contract is for 25 tonnes, what profit would you have made?**

   A $16,250

   B $1,125

   C $150

   D $15,750

72. **What is the purpose of assignment?**

   A   Trades are directed into the account of the beneficial owner

   B   Margin calls are made on the clearing members

   C   Buyers and sellers are not matched anonymously by the exchange

   D   Exchange members 'give up' a trade to a clearing firm

73. **The dominant trading system employed for NYSE Liffe commodity options is best described as**

   A   An open outcry market

   B   A Kerb market

   C   A Ring market

   D   An electronic order matching system

74. **Which of the following are regulated by the CFTC?**

 I Equities

 II Index options

 III Zinc futures

 IV Oil futures

A I and II

B II, III and IV

C III and IV

D III only

75. **What is the best description of the CFTC Part 30 exemption?**

A It allows resident US investors to trade on US exchanges

B It allows resident US investors to trade on non-US exchanges

C It allows non-resident US investors to trade on US exchanges

D It allows non-resident US investors to trade on non-US exchanges

Answers

1. **B**   The strategy is a synthetic long put. The maximum profit is the breakeven price, which will be strike minus cost of put option. The cost of the synthetic put will be

    P = S – C – K

       = Price of underlying – Call premium – Strike

       = 101 – 6 – 100 = (5)

    Therefore, the maximum profit is strike less premium = 100 – 5 = 95

    See Chapter 6 Section 3.2 and Chapter 1 Section 1.1.1 of your Study Text

2. **B**   Gearing is the ability to control an asset for less outlay than buying the underlying asset outright. For options this will be given by the premium or initial outlay relative to the price of the underlying asset or value of the contract.

    See Chapter 1, Section 2.1 of your Study Text

3. **C**   We have to assume that the Eurozone yield curve is normal (i.e. slightly upward sloping). Thus, a rotation with a flattening of the long term will mean that short-term interest rates are expected to rise in relation to long-term interest rates. Therefore, if short-term interest rates rise, the price of the Euribor future (100 minus the Eurozone interest rate) will fall so you will want to sell the Euribor future. If long-term interest rates are expected to fall then the price of Bunds will rise so you will want to buy the Bund future

    See Chapter 6, Section 4.2 of your Study Text

4. **A**   The question does not specify, but we are looking for a factor that increases both call and put premiums. An increase in interest rates and the price of the underlying would cause call premiums to rise, but cause put premiums to fall. An increase in the time to expiry and volatility will increase both put and call premiums

    See Chapter 3, Section 2.1 of your Study Text

5. **C**   In a contango market, futures prices are higher than cash prices

    See Chapter 3, Section 1.4.1 of your Study Text

6. **A**   An option is in-the-money if it has intrinsic value. A call option will have intrinsic value if the strike price is lower than the price of the underlying as by exercising the option, the investor can buy the underlying for a lower price than the market price

    See Chapter 3, Section 2.1 of your Study Text

7. **B**   The premium of a deeply in-the-money option will move in line with the underlying, giving a delta of 1

    See Chapter 3, Section 2.10 of your Study Text

8.   **C**   Going long the call and short the put gives a synthetic long with an initial debit of (30 – 20) 10 basis points. Hence, it will be the equivalent of a long future at the price of strike plus initial debit (i.e. 97.00 + 0.10). This can also be derived from the formula

$$C - P = S - K$$

$$S = C - P + K$$

$$= 0.30 - 0.20 + 97$$

$$= 97.10$$

The expression basis point represents the tick size of 1p per £100 nominal value

See Chapter 3, Section 2.8 of your Study Text

9.   **C**   Sell a collar. This means that e will sell a cap and buy a floor. Remember, by entering into these two trades, the depositor is expecting the premiums to offset each other. Hence he is protected at nil cost

See Chapter 4, Section 1.3 of your Study Text

10.   **C**   A stop order would allow the asset to be sold for less than 97, since the stop order becomes a market order once the price is touched. The question indicates that the investor would be willing to sell for more than 97 rather than less than 97, so a stop limit order is appropriate

See Chapter 3, Section 4.2 of your Study Text

11.   **A**   Buying a horizontal call spread involves buying the near dated call option and selling the far dated call option both with the same strike price. As both options have the same strike this is a delta neutral strategy i.e. it is unaffected by a change in the market price. The investor is selling the longer dated option which has the greater volatility value and buying the short dated option with less volatility value. Therefore he will profit if volatility falls. Remember vertical spreads relate to changes in price, horizontal spreads to changes in volatility

See Chapter 6, Section 3.11 of your Study Text

12.   **A**   A cross trade is where a firm buys from one client and then sells on to another client, acting as intermediary and counterparty for both trades

See Chapter 3, Section 4.1 of your Study Text

13.   **D**   Novation is a very important process by which LCH.Clearnet acts as central counterparty to all trades. It creates liquidity in the market and allows investors to close out positions more easily

See Chapter 5, Section 1.2 of your Study Text

14.   **C**   C is a synthetic long. In fact, all of the trades given are speculative, but the risk of A, B and D are limited to option premiums, whereas the risk of the synthetic long is large but limited (almost unlimited). Hence, C is the most speculative trade, which we assume therefore makes it the best available answer

See Chapter 6, Section 3.2 of your Study Text

15.   **B**   For options on futures traded on NYSE Liffe, the premium is paid on close and so long option positions are margined as well as short option positions

See Chapter 5, Section 2.5.1 of your Study Text

16. **A** A trick question, while the mechanics involve entering into a 'received fixed swap; the act of changing a FRN into what is effectively a fixed rate bond is better described as an 'asset swap'

    See Chapter 4, Section 1.8 of your Study Text

17. **A** The existing position is a synthetic long call. To eliminate market risk a synthetic short call is required, which can be constructed with a short put and short underlying

    See Chapter 6, Section 3.2 of your Study Text

18. **B** Bullish positions i.e. long calls and short puts have positive deltas. An increase in the delta will make a bullish position more profitable and a bearish position more loss-making. Therefore the short call might need to put up more variation margin. Since equity options pay premium upfront there would be no corresponding decrease in margin applicable for the long call

    See Chapter 3, Section 2.10 of your Study Text

19. **B** Arrears. All the others have national principal which rises or falls over the life of the contract

    See Chapter 4, Section 3.4 of your Study Text

20. **A** The correct name for a currency swap whereby both parties pay a floating rate is a 'cross currency basis swap'

    See Chapter 4, Section 1.5 of your Study Text

21. **D** I   If interest rates rise, the price of bonds such as gilts will fall, thus benefiting the short future

    II   The seller of a bond future is expecting prices to fall NOT rise

    III   The STIR future is an interest rate future, so will not offset the long gilt future

    IV   The bond future is physically delivered using one of a basket of deliverable gilts

    See Chapter 6, Section 4.1 of your Study Text

22. **C** The return from the cash and carry for each of the gilts in the basket of deliverable gilts is known as the implied repo rate. The gilt with the highest implied repo rate is the cheapest-to-deliver gilt. It will not necessarily be the cheapest gilt, as this will not necessarily yield the highest return on a cash and carry arbitrage

    See Chapter 6, Section 4.1.2 of your Study Text

23. **B** Total return swap

    See Chapter 4, Section 1.8 of your Study Text

24. **D** Maturity is desired. Failure of the credit instrument to mature as expected is what is being protected against

    See Chapter 4, Section 1.9 of your Study Text

25. **B** CFTC Part 30 (foreign futures and options) relates to a US person trading via a non-US firm on a non-US exchange. It is a US regulation designed to provide protection for US persons no matter where they currently reside. In order to be able to do this, the non-US firm must secure exemption from Part 30

    See Chapter 7, Section 2.4 of your Study Text

26. **A** A call option is out-of-the-money when the underlying asset is less than the strike. A put option is out-of-the-money when the underlying asset is greater than the strike. The option premium is irrelevant

See Chapter 1, Sections 1.11 and 1.13 of your Study Text

27. **A** The other answers are examples of credit events

See Chapter 4, Section 1.10 of your Study Text

28. **D** The main reason why investors trade on exchange is that LCH.Clearnet novates the trade and effectively eliminates counterparty risk

See Chapter 5, Section 1.2 of your Study Text

29. **B** Cash or physically

See Chapter 4, Sections 1.9 and 3.1 of your Study Text

30. **A** Credit spread put option

See Chapter 4, Section 3.1 of your Study Text

31. **D** If the market rises, the loss on the short underlying position will be offset by the gain on the long call, hedging the short underlying position. This is similar to hedging a long position by buying put options

See Chapter 6, Section 3.1 of your Study Text

32. **A** Index future fair value will equal the cash price + cost of carry. The cost of carry will be a factor of the market yield and interest rates

See Chapter 3, Section 1.3 of your Study Text

33. **C** No reduction will be allowed since both the September and December positions are long

See Chapter 5, Section 2.6.3 of your Study Text

34. **B** A   If short-term interest rates are less than the dividend or coupon received from holding the asset, there will be a net benefit of carry and the future will be at a discount to the cash price (i.e. there will be a negative cost of carry)

   B   Only a long hedge will benefit from basis weakening. If we assume the cash price remains constant, the long future in the hedge will be closed out by selling a future at a higher price if basis has weakened

   C   If you sell an intramarket spread, you are selling the near-dated future and buying the long-dated. If the cost of carry increases, the price of the long-dated future will increase more than the price of the short-dated future

   D   A contango market is a normal market, with a net cost of carry which will mean that longer dated futures would be expected to be at a premium to short-dated futures

See Chapter 3, Section 1.5 of your Study Text

35. **B**   The name of the spread is given by what the investor is doing with the near-dated future. Hence, in this case, buying the spread

If the spread is +25 (assuming this is basis points), and remembering the inverse price relationship between interest rates and the future price, it must be that shorter term interest rates are lower than longer term. For example, if near-dated interest rates were 5% the STIR price would be 95, whereas the longer dated interest rate expectations of 5.25% would give a STIR price of 94.75. Hence the spread of the near-dated (95) minus the far-dated (94.75) would give +25 basis points

In other words, we have a normal yield curve. If the investor has bought the spread he must expect the near-dated future to rise and, hence, near interest rates to fall. Conversely, he must expect the far future to fall and, hence, for interest rates to rise. In other words, he expects the yield curve to steepen

See Chapter 6, Section 4.2 of your Study Text

36. **B**   Bermudan, American and European all have fixed strike prices set at the beginning of the contract. They do, however, have differences in terms of exercise flexibility

See Chapter 4, Section 5.1 of your Study Text

37. **B**   Three-month future fair value = $100 + 3 × $10 = $130
Four-month future fair value = $100 + 4 × $10 = $140
Five-month future fair value = $100 + 5 × $10 = $150
Six-month future fair value = $100 + 6 × $10 = $160

Therefore, the three-month and six-month futures are not trading at their fair value and represent an arbitrage opportunity

See Chapter 3, Section 1.3 of your Study Text

38. **C**   Selling a call and a put with the same strike and expiry gives a short straddle (assume the expiry is the same unless told otherwise). The breakeven points are strike plus or minus both premiums, i.e. 100 +/– 12

See Chapter 6, Section 3.7.3 of your Study Text

39. **D**   A swaption is the option to enter into a swap rather than an obligation to enter into one. A payer swap is when you pay fixed rate and receive floating rate. Therefore, if you are buying the right to lock into a fixed rate, you are hedging against interest rates rising, but not necessarily locking in a rate

See Chapter 4, Section 1.4.2 of your Study Text

40. **C**   Options are more flexible and, when used for hedging, leave potential for profit if the price rises. However, they are more expensive since the holder has to pay premium. The short hedge (selling a future) is the cheaper method

See Chapter 6, Section 3.1 of your Study Text

41. **A**   Although swaps do exist in relation to currency risk, credit risk and equity risk, the question explicitly states that it is an interest rate swap. Therefore, we must assume that the client has borrowed at a comparatively favourable rate in either fixed or floating and then swapped the loan to their preferred rate format. They will, therefore, have cheaper finance than if they had just borrowed in their original preferred format

See Chapter 4, Section 1.4 of your Study Text

42. **D** $\dfrac{\text{Nominal value of CTD}}{\text{Nominal value of future}} \times \text{Price factor of CTD}$

See Chapter 6, Section 4.1.3 of your Study Text

43. **B** Calculate fair value of one-year FTSE 100 future

= Cash index × (Finance charge – Dividend yield)

= 5000 × (4.5% – 3%)

= 5075

Therefore, the future is trading above its fair value and you want to buy the cash and sell the future (cash and carry arbitrage). Selling the future on its own is not sufficient as it is the relative mispricing between the cash and future that you want to exploit

See Chapter 3, Sections 1.3 and 1.6 of your Study Text

44. **C** Buying futures on the index will mean that the fund will perform in accordance with that index. The part of the fund that is not being used to fund the margin requirement of the future should be held as cash or cash equivalents

See Chapter 6, Section 7.7 of your Study Text

45. **B** LIBOR rises

See Chapter 4, Section 1.2 of your Study Text

46. **D** Deeply out-of-the-money call options have a strike a long way above the underlying price; and a delta close to zero. They offer the buyer a remote chance of profit and hence, the premiums will be low and liquidity will be limited

See Chapter 3, Section 2 of your Study Text

47. **A** Buyer and sellers of futures are always margined. Sellers of options are always margined but buyers of options are not margined if they pay the premium 'up front'

See Chapter 5, Section 2.5.1 of your Study Text

48. **C** Most derivative trading is now electronic screen based, allowing exchange price feeds to obtain live prices direct from these trading systems

See Chapter 3, Section 3.1.3 of your Study Text

49. **B** The variation margin (loss) will equal the adverse movement. The initial margin remains at 5% until the contract is closed, when it will be returned to the investor

See Chapter 5, Section 3.5 of your Study Text

50. **A** The contract for difference is cash settled and the final settlement will be the final variation margin payment, i.e. the final mark to market. An index product is an example, not a description of a contract for difference

See Chapter 1, Section 1.6.1 of your Study Text

51. **D** As you are long futures, you will close out by selling futures. A stop limit order will not be executed at $865, as this is a worse price at which to sell than the $875 limit

See Chapter 3, Section 4.2.5 of your Study Text

52. **A** Although the hedger will be looking at the cash and futures prices, there will be no risk to him as long as they move together. The risk that the hedger has is if the difference between the cash and the futures prices change, i.e. if the basis changes

   See Chapter 3, Section 1.5.2 of your Study Text

53. **B** The position created is a long strangle, as it is constructed with options of different strikes. The breakeven points are the upper strike plus both premiums, and the lower strike minus both premiums

   See Chapter 6, Section 3.7.4 of your Study Text

54. **A** This is the best available answer in that segregation must always be provided for US citizens and you may trade US products if NFA registered. If your firm has not been exempted from CFTC Part 30, the US domiciled citizen cannot trade UK exchange contracts

   See Chapter 7, Section 2.4 of your Study Text

55. **B** Clearing is the general term for all LCH.Clearnet activities. Novation just relates to the guarantee part due to LCH.Clearnet acting as a central counterparty for all trades

   See Chapter 5, Section 1.2 of your Study Text

56. **C** Remember that basis trades must be reported within 15 minutes

   See Chapter 3, Section 3.1.1 of your Study Text

57. **C** With currency swaps, principals are chosen to be approximately equivalent

   See Chapter 4, Sections 1.5 and 3.4 of your Study Text

58. **D** Both long and short futures positions will be margined, and both initial and variation margin is required. Options on futures on the LME are an exception to this since the premium is paid up front

   See Chapter 5, Section 2.5.1 of your Study Text

59. **A** One way to try and remember the difference between the US regulators for the exam may be that the **SEC** regulates

   Securities (i.e. the NYSE)

   Equity derivatives (i.e. S&P 500 futures and options and the exchanges they trade on, e.g. CBO**E**)

   Currencies (e.g. CME currency futures and PHLX currency options)

   whereas the **CFT**C regulates **C**ommodity derivatives and **T**-bond futures

   See Chapter 7, Section 2.2 of your Study Text

60. **B** An arbitrage opportunity is the opportunity to make risk-free profit

    A   If the FTSE 100 future goes down whilst the value of the constituent stock goes up, it suggests that there is a mispricing between the underlying and the future and hence, there is an arbitrage opportunity

    B   Buying a call with a view to the underlying asset rising is a speculative trade, not an arbitrage opportunity

    C   If the price of the constituent legs of a spread trade differs from the market's bid offer for the spread itself, e.g. if you can construct a bull spread by buying a low strike call and selling a high-strike call for a different price to selling the spread then again there is an arbitrage opportunity

    D   If the price of the synthetic position differs from the futures price, there is the opportunity to do either a reversal or a conversion arbitrage trade

See Chapter 1, Section 1.11 of your Study Text

61. **B** Hedging is the process of reducing risk, such as the farmer going short the wheat future to hedge their underlying long wheat position. The process of exploiting a mispricing is known as arbitrage. The deposit of collateral to protect against credit risk is known as margining

See Chapter 6, Section 3 of your Study Text

62. **C** Gamma is defined as the rate of change of delta with respect to a change in the price of the underlying so C is the best answer. A and D are features of Gamma but do not define it. B is a pure distractor

See Chapter 3, Section 2.11 of your Study Text

63. **D** Although basis would represent the amount by which the future's price exceeds the cash price in a contango market, this is not the best definition of basis. Basis would also occur in a backwardation market. Therefore, the best definition explains how to arrive at basis in both a backwardation and contango market by deducting the future's price from the cash price

See Chapter 3, Section 1.5.1 of your Study Text

64. **B** Net delta = 3 × -1 (delta of short future)

                = −7 + 4 × -1 (delta of deeply ITM puts)

See Chapter 3, Section 2.10 of your Study Text

65. **C** This is a vertical bull spread constructed with calls and an initial debit trade. Therefore the maximum profit is given by the difference in strikes minus the difference in the premiums

See Chapter 6, Section 3.3 of your Study Text

66. **D** Open outcry is also known as floor trading and is transparent as it is possible to see (and hear) exactly what prices are being made by everyone, not just those prices on your particular screen. If it were 24-hour trading, you'd have some pretty tired floor traders!

See Chapter 2, Section 2.1 of your Study Text

67. **B**   A short straddle would be suitable if both call and put volatility was expected to fall. As only call volatility is expected to fall, the horizontal spread is the most appropriate

See Chapter 6, Section 3.11 of your Study Text

68. **B**   The SEC regulates some areas of derivatives but is mainly a securities regulator

See Chapter 7, Section 2.2 of your Study Text

69. **D**   The speculator was bullish: the price went up, not down and hence, a profit was made. Without the tick size, we cannot apply our usual profit/loss formula, so we need to improvise

		$	$
Buy ten tonnes (two contracts)	@ 790		(7,900)
Sell ten tonnes	@ 820		8,200
Profit			300

See Chapter 6, Section 1.3 of your Study Text

70. **C**   A long floor is the best answer. However this will have a cost. The investor might, instead, also sell a cap (short cap) to create a collar. This can be done at little or no cost

See Chapter 4, Section 1.3 of your Study Text

71. **D**

	$
Profit = ($2,775 − $2,710) × 25 tonnes × ten contracts	16,250
Less commission (ten contracts @ $50)	(500)
	15,750

The term 'round turn' incorporates the cost of both buying and selling

See Chapter 6, Section 1.3 of your Study Text

72. **A**   The 'giving up' of trades is known as allocation, not assignment. The term assignment is when trades are recorded to the correct house or individual client account

See Chapter 3, Section 5.3 of your Study Text

73. **D**   Open outcry is often referred to as floor trading. On the LME, the floor is called the Ring and during market hours, specific metals trade at specific times in the Ring. Outside of these times, trading occurs outside of the Ring; this is referred to as Kerb trading. On NYSE Liffe Commodity Products, open outcry is no longer used; all trading is executed on LIFFE CONNECT, the exchange's electronic order matching system

See Chapter 2, Section 2.3 of your Study Text

74. **C**   The CFTC regulates all of the commodity markets. The SEC is responsible for regulating the equity derivatives

See Chapter 7, Sections 2.2 and 2.3 of your Study Text

75. **B** The CFTC Part 30 Exemption protects US resident citizens when trading outside the US. Firms outside the US may only do business with US resident citizens if they have the Part 30 Exemption which provides the US customers with a basic level of protection even when trading offshore (e.g. the right to sue in the US courts, seek arbitration from the US regulator and get the US version of the warrant and derivative risk warning – the CFTC risk disclosure)

See Chapter 7, Section 2.4 of your Study Text

Practice Examination 2

75 Questions in 1 hour 30 minutes

1. **Which of the following contracts are legally binding?**

   A   Master agreement

   B   Confirmation

   C   Neither master agreement or confirmation

   D   Both master agreement and confirmation

2. **How would you construct a short strangle?**

   A   Short call and short put at the same strikes

   B   Short call and short put at different strikes

   C   Short low-strike put and short high-strike put

   D   Short high-strike call and short low-strike call

3. **If short-term interest rates were expected to fall, what effect would this have on the spread between two delivery months on a futures contract with an underlying asset in good supply?**

   A   Widen

   B   Narrow

   C   Remain unchanged

   D   Indeterminate

4. **Who uses an independent guarantee?**

   A   The Exchange

   B   LCH. Clearnet

   C   Member firms

   D   Clearing Members

5. **In bond futures contracts that allow delivery on any business day in the delivery month, why would delivery take place early?**

   A   The seller elects to deliver because yields exceed short-term interest rates

   B   The seller elects to deliver because short-term rates exceed yields

   C   The buyer elects to deliver because yields exceed short-term interest rates

   D   The buyer elects to deliver because short-term rates exceed yields

6. **A change in basis is profitable for the short hedger if**

    A   Cash price goes down while futures remain steady

    B   Cash prices move from a premium over to a discount under futures

    C   Futures price goes down while the cash price remains unchanged

    D   Cash and futures move in unison

7. **What is the main purpose of the TRS?**

    A   Registration of trades

    B   Settlement

    C   Clearing

    D   Trade reporting

8. **A futures spreader who anticipates short-term supply tightness in the underlying asset would consider**

    A   Selling the futures spread

    B   Buying the futures spread

    C   No action, since it is impossible to calculate the spread risk

    D   None of the above

9. **What does ISDA stand for?**

    A   International Swaps and Derivatives Association

    B   International Swaps Documentation Association

    C   International Settlement of Derivatives Association

    D   International Standards for derivatives Association

10. **List the three bonds in descending order, according to their likely price factors.**

    The three bonds eligible for delivery in the gilt future are

    >   I   Treasury 8% 2011

    >   II   Treasury 10% 2011

    >   III   Conversion 9.5% 2012

    A   I, II, III

    B   II, III, I

    C   III, II, I

    D   II, I, III

11.   **What would be the variation margin in the following trade?**

An index point is worth $10

Sell 14 futures at 1382

Settlement price on day of trade = 1369

A $130

B $170

C $1,820

D $2,380

12.   **What would be the fair value of a 180-day gold future, assuming adequate supply and given the following information?**

Cash price $330 per oz, interest rates 3% and insurance costs of $1 per oz per month

A $334.95 per oz

B $339.90 per oz

C $340.95 per oz

D $351.90 per oz

13.   **A synthetic short call is created by which of the following trades?**

A   Buy future, buy put

B   Sell future, sell put

C   Sell future, buy call

D   Buy future, sell call

14.   **If an investor bought a June 100 call for 22 and sold a June 120 call for 6, what market view would he have?**

A   Neutral

B   Volatile

C   Bullish

D   Bearish

15.   **If you were bullish about an asset's price, which two of the following trades would you undertake?**

I   Write call

II   Buy call

III   Write put

IV   Buy put

A   I and II

B   II and III

C   I and IV

D   II and IV

16. **An investor wants to sell when the market reaches a trigger below the current level. They are prepared to sell higher, but not lower than this trigger. Which is the best order to place to reflect this view?**

   A Stop order

   B Stop limit

   C Guaranteed stop

   D Sell MIT

17. **The current fair value of an asset is £31. The risk-free rate is 10%. The premium on a 30 strike call is £3 and on a 30 strike put is £1. Both options expire in one year. Which of the following strategies should be used?**

   A Buy call and sell put

   B Sell call and buy put

   C Buy call and buy put

   D Sell call and sell put

18. **What is the name of a margin call made by a bank to its counterparty?**

   A Return amount

   B Delivery amount

   C Collateral

   D Variation margin

19. **When a trade is registered with LCH.Clearnet where does the risk lie?**

   A It still lies with the broker

   B The broker is relieved from risk

   C The risk is split between the broker and LCH.Clearnet

   D The risk is assigned to the Clearing Member

20. **When are confirmations normally agreed using Market Wire?**

   A T + 0

   B T + 1

   C T + 3

   D T + 10

21. **How many bond futures would be traded to hedge an anticipated holding of €50m nominal of the cheapest-to-deliver bond? The contract size is €250,000 and the price factor of the CTD is 1.112233, the notional coupon is 6%.**

   A 180

   B 200

   C 222

   D 247

22. **What happens to the premium on an out of the money put option if the price of the underlying rises?**

   A   No change

   B   Increase

   C   Decrease

   D   It depends on whether the premium is settled up front or on exercise

23. **Under which of the following systems can novation occur?**

   A   MarkitWire

   B   SwapClear

   C   DTCC

   D   SWIFT

24. **You sell a FTSE 100 call option with an exercise price of 6050. The premium is 50 index points. At what index level at expiry would you begin to lose money?**

   A   As soon as the underlying rises above 6050

   B   As soon as the underlying falls below 6050

   C   As soon as the underlying rises above 6100

   D   As soon as the underlying falls below 6000

25. **An in-the-money call means that**

   A   The strike of the call is below the market

   B   The strike of the call is above the market

   C   The strike is close to the market

   D   All of the above

26. **How is gearing measured?**

   A   Market value of contract as percentage of nominal value

   B   Nominal value of contract divided by initial outlay

   C   Nominal value of contract divided by market value

   D   Market value of contract divided by initial outlay

27. **An investor who is short a FTSE future can best protect his position from a temporary rise in the stock market by**

   A   Buying a FTSE put

   B   Writing a FTSE put

   C   Writing a FTSE call

   D   Any of the above

28. **A short futures hedge is preferable to a hedge using puts because**

A The short hedge retains upside potential

B The futures hedge is more flexible

C The futures hedge is cheaper

D The futures hedge has no basis risk

---

29. **It is June and a trader observes that the NYSE Liffe September gilt future is 102.10 and the December future is 103.25. He expects that the spread will widen. He should**

A Buy September and sell December

B Buy September and buy December

C Sell September and buy December

D Sell September and sell December

---

30. **A US equity fund manager wants to hedge a $15m portfolio which tracks the S&P 500. The S&P future is at 1125 and the contract is $500 an index point. How many futures are required for the hedge?**

A 300

B 54

C 27

D 13

---

31. **Responsibility for regulating US Treasury bill futures is in the hands of**

A US Treasury

B Federal Reserve

C SEC

D CFTC

---

32. **Which of the following would constitute a collar?**

A Long swap short swaption

B Long receiver swaption short payer swaption

C Long cap, long floor

D Long cap, short floor

---

33. **An MIT order, entered before the market opens, to sell three futures at 18.50 MIT GTC**

A Would be executed if the market opened at 18.60

B Would be executed if the market opens at 18.50

C Could be filled at 18.40

D All the above are correct

---

34. **If LCH.Clearnet see that a member has built up a large position in a particular contract and are worried they will not be able to meet their financial commitments, what can they do?**

    A   Force the firm to close all of their positions

    B   Move all of their positions to other member firms

    C   Stop the firm from trading

    D   Impose a trading halt on that product on the exchange

35. **What would be the approximate fair value of a FTSE 100 index future, if interest rates are 6%, dividend yield 4% cash, FTSE is 4130 and there are 60 days until delivery?**

    A   4171

    B   4116

    C   4144

    D   4089

36. **The exercise of a long call on a long gilt futures contract will require the exercising long to assume a**

    A   Long position in gilts

    B   Long position in long gilt futures

    C   Short position in gilts

    D   Short position in long gilt futures

37. **An open position in a stock index futures contract, if held to maturity, would be settled by**

    A   Delivery or receipt of actual securities

    B   Cash settlement, based on the contract's total monetary value

    C   Cash settlement, based on difference between the final settlement price and the previous day's close

    D   Interexchange depository receipt for listed securities

38. **Who is responsible for reporting a trade conducted on LIFFE CONNECT?**

    A   Buyer

    B   Seller

    C   Neither party needs to report

    D   Both parties must report

39. **To liquidate a short position in gilt futures when the price falls below a price that is below the prevailing market, a trader would tell his broker to use a**

    A   Sell MIT order

    B   Buy limit order

    C   Buy stop order

    D   Sell stop order

40. A borrower is paying a fixed rate of interest and expects interest rates to fall. What swap should he enter into?

A Fixed for floating

B Floating for fixed

C Basis swap

D Total return swap

41. The current portfolio is short ten calls (call delta = 0.4). How can this portfolio be made delta neutral?

A Buy four futures

B Buy ten futures

C Sell ten futures

D Sell four futures

42. An investor has bought a 740 equity index straddle. If the underlying is standing at 766, how much is the intrinsic value on the call option?

A 0

B 766

C Depends on the premiums

D 26

43. Which of the following structured products is best described as a loan with an embedded put option?

A Callable bond

B Convertible bond

C Putable bond

D Index-linked bond

44. What was a reason for the OTC market to become established?

A To increase liquidity

B To trade standardised contracts

C To be able to hedge more accurately

D To be centrally cleared

45. Where might you expect time value to be greatest amongst the following options? The underlying is at 120.

A 160 call

B 140 call

C 120 call

D 100 call

46. **Which of the following would not be covered in a master agreement?**

   A Termination events

   B Events of default

   C Specific terms of each deal

   D Payment netting

47. **Which of the following are instruments that may not be used to hedge interest rate exposure?**

   A Short-term interest rate futures

   B Interest rate caps

   C S&P 500 future

   D Forward rate agreements

48. **The Commodity Futures Modernization Act 2000 does which two of the following?**

       I   Prohibits the trading of single-stock futures

       II   Removes the prohibition on the trading of single-stock futures

       III   Makes most OTC derivative contracts legally enforceable

       IV   Makes most OTC derivative contracts legally unenforceable

   A I and III

   B I and IV

   C II and III

   D II and IV

49. **A customer provides initial margin to the broker of £10,000 and the customer agreement has a trigger level of £8,000. Variation margin payments reduce the balance down to £7,750. Which of the following is true?**

   A The customer will be required to top up the margin by £250

   B The customer will be required to top up the margin by £2,250

   C The customer will be required to submit a payment of 10% of the initial margin

   D The customer will be required to close out the position

50. **The best definition of gamma is**

   A The rate of change of an option's delta with respect to its underlying

   B The rate of change of the underlying with respect to its premium

   C The rate of change of an option's premium with respect to its underlying

   D The rate of change of the underlying with respect to its delta

51. **What is the main difference between variation margin and initial margin?**

A   Initial margin is always returned

B   Variation margin must always be cash

C   Collateral given as initial margin will be subject to less of a haircut than the same collateral given as variation margin

D   UK government bonds denominated in euros are not acceptable collateral as initial margin

52. **Which of the following is the key characteristic of a credit derivative?**

A   It protects against a credit downgrade

B   It allows the investor to sell a bond in the market at a pre-agreed price

C   It allows the issuer to buy a bond back at an agreed price

D   It is a method of hedging interest rate exposure for a borrower

53. **An MIT order, entered before the market opens to sell ten STIR futures at 94.00 MIT GD**

A   Would not be cancelled at the end of the day it is entered, if not executed

B   Would be executed if the market opens at 93.00

C   Could be filled at a price of 97.10

D   All of the above are correct

54. **If you were to buy a March 100 call and sell a March 100 put, which of the following trades would you have undertaken?**

A   Long straddle

B   Short straddle

C   Long strangle

D   Synthetic long

55. **Which of the following swaps would not be eligible for the SwapClear system?**

A   10 year AUD

B   30 year USD

C   5 year NZD

D   20 year GBP

56. **What is the main purpose of DTCC's Deriv/SERV system?**

A   Clearing

B   Matching

C   Settlement

D   Trading

57. **Which of the following is the best description of a plain vanilla swaption?**

    A   The exchange of a fixed rate option for a floating rate option

    B   The right, but not the obligation, to enter into a swap agreement

    C   The right, but not the obligation, to include the exchange of principal in addition to interest rates within a swap agreement

    D   The exchange of interest rates based on one currency for interest rates based on another currency

58. **The SEC regulates which exchange?**

    A   CBOT

    B   CBOE

    C   NYMEX

    D   CME

59. **Which TWO of the following exchanges have common trading and settlement links that allow identical contracts to be opened on one market and closed on the other?**

    A   CME and Osaka

    B   NYSE Liffe and CME

    C   CBOT and EUREX

    D   CME and SGX

60. **Which of the following best describes a contango market?**

    A   A market where the near prices are higher than far prices

    B   A market where the far prices are higher than near prices

    C   A market where prices are constant

    D   A market where the prices increase or decrease by a constant amount

61. **What is the value of the FTSE 100 index option?**

    A   £10 per tick

    B   £10 per index point

    C   £10 per contract

    D   £1 per index point

62. **When do you have to pay an option premium after buying an equity option on NYSE Liffe?**

    A   Trade day

    B   Next business day

    C   Two business days following the trade

    D   On exercise

63. **An investor wishing to profit from a change in the spread between dollar and sterling interest rates might undertake which of the following trades?**

    A Basis swap

    B Plain vanilla swap

    C FRA

    D Sell STIR futures

64. **Germany has just found oil deposits in the Baltic. Japan is having severe labour problems. To take advantage of the expected currency fluctuations, you would**

    A Sell euro futures

    B Buy yen futures

    C Buy euro/sell yen futures

    D Sell euro/buy yen futures

65. **If an investor enters into the following trade, what would be his motivation?**

    Long October 310 Tesco call at a premium of 12

    Sell December 310 Tesco call at a premium of 15

    A Exploiting a rise in volatility

    B Speculating on a bullish market

    C Exploiting time decay

    D Speculating on a bearish market

66. **A short-term interest rate future is the exchange-traded equivalent of which OTC product?**

    A Overnight deposit

    B IRS

    C FRA

    D Three-month Eurodollar options

67. **Calculate the points at which the following trade would break even.**

    Sell 4700 FTSE 100 call at a premium of 76

    Sell 4600 FTSE 100 put at a premium of 35

    A 4624 and 4635

    B 4811 and 4489

    C 4776 and 4565

    D 4511 and 4711

68. Why do hedgers find futures contracts most useful?

A   They can beat speculators in reacting to important market news

B   They can ensure that someone else pays for any losses they incur

C   They can bring a degree of certainty to their future cash flows

D   They can deal in and out quickly for profit at low dealing costs

69. Which of the following is not a type of swap?

A   FRN

B   CMS

C   TRS

D   OIS

70. The cocoa futures price moves by 75 ticks. Given what the tick value is £10 what will the profit or loss be for an investor who has bought 5 contracts?

A   £375

B   £3,750

C   £1,875

D   £750

71. Which of the following is an advantage of principles based regulation?

A   It has decreased flexibility

B   Less scope for interpretation of the regulations in certain situations

C   It has well defined rules that apply in all situations

D   It is more applicable to client-based services

72. Who provides information to quote vendors in an open outcry system?

A   Market officials

B   Pit observers

C   Clearing members

D   Trade members

73. Which of the following would be the best description of a market that is in backwardation?

A   The futures price is not trading at its fair value

B   It is possible to agree to buy the asset for delivery at a future date at a lower price than the asset is currently trading in the cash market

C   The price of the synthetic position is trading above the underlying asset leading to a risk-free profit opportunity through trading the reversal

D   The futures price is trading above the cash price

74. **An American importer places an order with a German car manufacturer. The order to be delivered in August is valued at €10m. The spot price for the euro is 1.2675 and September futures are trading at 1.2625. The most effective hedge would be**

    A   Buy spot euro and sell euro futures

    B   Sell spot euro and buy euro futures

    C   Buy euro futures

    D   Sell euro futures

75. **Which of the following is the best description of an order that is marked GTC?**

    A   The order will remain on the broker's order book until the end of the trading day

    B   The order may not be executed unless the minimum or maximum price stated has been triggered by a trade in the market

    C   The order will remain good until the broker receives further instruction from the client

    D   The order must be exercised in the closing session of the market

Answers

1. **D** Both master agreement and confirmation

   See Chapter 4, Section 2.1 and 2.3 of your Study Text

2. **B** A strangle is a combination trade, so you need to combine a call with a put. As it is a strangle, the call and put must have different strikes

   See Chapter 6, Section 3.7.6 of your Study Text

3. **B** The cost of carry would fall due to the lower interest rate, thus the difference between the two fair values would be narrower

   See Chapter 3, Section 1.2 and 1.3 of your Study Text

4 **C** LCH. Clearnet uses a mutual guarantee structure in order to guarantee the trades of clearing members with each other. Member firms provide an independent guarantee to their clients – i.e. the clients only have recourse to resources of the member firm they traded with in the event of insolvency

   See Chapter 5, Section 1.3 of your Study Text

5. **B** Rational sellers will always deliver at a time which best suits them. Consequently, if short-term interest rates are higher than the yield on the bond, there will be merit in delivering as early as possible, receive the cash and invest it at a better rate than the bond yield

   See Chapter 6, Section 4.1.5 of your Study Text

6. **C** The short hedger has sold the future and holds the physical asset. Therefore, they will benefit if they can close out their position by buying back the future at a lower price whilst still getting the same cash price

   See Chapter 6, Section 3.8 of your Study Text

7. **A** As suggested by the name TRS (Trade Registration System). The TRS can be thought of as the electronic back office system of NYSE Liffe that prepares a trade executed on LIFFE .connect for registration at the clearing house by undertaking the procedures of matching, assignment and allocation (give-up)

   See Chapter 3, Section 5.1 of your Study Text

8. **B** Short-term supply tightness will lead to an increase in the near-dated future relative to the long-dated. Therefore, the investor should buy the near-dated and sell the far-dated, i.e. buying the spread

   See Chapter 6, Section 2.1 of your Study Text

9. **A** International Swaps and Derivatives Association

   See Chapter 4, Section 2 of your Study Text

10. **B** A higher coupon for approximately the same maturity bond will mean a higher market value which will result in a higher price factor

   See Chapter 6, Section 4.1.1 of your Study Text

11. **C**   13 index points at $10 per point × 14 contracts = $1,820

See Chapter 5, Section 2.5 of your Study Text

12. **C**

	$
Cash price	330.00
Cost of carry	
Interest: $330 × 3% × $\frac{180}{360}$	4.95
Insurance: 6 × $1	6.00
	$340.95

See Chapter 3, Section 1.3 of your Study Text

13. **B**   A synthetic short call is created by simultaneously selling a future and selling a put

See Chapter 6, Section 3.2 of your Study Text

14. **C**   A bull call spread as they have bought the low strike and sold the high strike

See Chapter 6, Section 3.3 of your Study Text

15. **B**   Look for the bullish trades: long call and short put. The bearish trades would be short call and long put

See Chapter 1, Sections 1.11, 1.12, 1.13 and 1.14 of your Study Text

16. **B**   The stop limit order combines the sell stop with a limit order, such that once triggered the order will not be filled at any price below the trigger, but could be filled above

See Chapter 3, Section 4.2.5 of your Study Text

17. **A**   The fair value of the one-year future would be the cash price plus the cost of carry

FV = £31 + (0.1 × £31) = £34.10

The synthetic long would be

C − P + K (£3 − £1 + £30) = £32

Therefore, the strategy would be the reversal, i.e. buy the call and sell the put (synthetic long) and sell the future

See Chapter 3, Sections 2.8 and 2.9 of your Study Text

18. **B**   In the margining of OTC contracts, the margin demanded is called the 'delivery amount'

See Chapter 4, Section 6.8 of your Study Text

19. **B**   Novation takes place at registration so that the risk lies with LCH.Clearnet i.e. the broker is relieved of the risk

See Chapter 2, Section 3 of your Study Text

20. **A**   MarkitWire is a trade affirmation/confirmation system

See Chapter 4, Section 6.1 of your Study Text

21. C $\dfrac{\text{Nominal value of holding}}{\text{Nominal value of future}} \times PF_{CTD}$

$\dfrac{€50m}{€0.25m} \times 1.112233 = 222$ contracts

See Chapter 6, Section 4.1.3 of your Study Text

22. C   As the price of the underlying rises, the right to sell at a fixed price becomes less attractive, i.e. the option goes even more out-of-the-money and premiums fall

See Chapter 3, Section 2 of your Study Text

23. B   LCH.Clearnet becomes the central counterparty to each party to the trade

See Chapter 4, Section 6.2 of your Study Text

24. C   The breakeven price for a call option is the exercise price plus the premium

See Chapter 1, Section 1.12 of your Study Text

25. A   Options that are in-the-money have intrinsic value, thus for a call, the strike must be below the current market price of the asset. You could then buy the asset at the lower price and quickly resell it at the higher price, thus realising a profit

See Chapter 3, Section 2.4 of your Study Text

26.   B   A strange question given that there is no 'official' calculation of gearing in this context. However it is the relationship between the size of the potential profits or losses (which will relate to the nominal value of the contract) and the initial outlay which is important

See Chapter 1, Section 2.1 of your Study Text

27. B   The put premium will partly offset the losses. The long put and short call are both bearish trades and thus will increase losses if the FTSE rises

See Chapter 6, Section 8.1 of your Study Text

28. C   Options are more flexible, but also more expensive as a premium will have to be paid. There is no premium payable entering into a futures contract

See Chapter 6, Section 3.1 of your Study Text

29. C   He needs an intramarket spread (buy one and sell another). If the spread widens, he should sell near and buy far (i.e. sell the spread)

See Chapter 6, Section 2.1 of your Study Text

30. C $\dfrac{\$15m}{1,125 \times \$500} = 26.67$ (round to 27)

See Chapter 6, Section 3.10 of your Study Text

31. D   The SEC only looks after equity derivatives

See Chapter 7, Section 2.2 of your Study Text

32. D   Long cap, short floor

See Chapter 4, Section 1.3 of your Study Text

33. **D** A sell MIT order is entered **above** the current market price. It therefore becomes a market order if 18.50 is reached or exceeded. As a market order, it could be filled at any price

See Chapter 3, Section 4.2.6 of your Study Text

34. **A** LCH.Clearnet would just close out the positions to prevent future losses hoping that the collateral held as initial margins would be sufficient to cover the close out losses

See Chapter 5, Section 1.5 of your Study Text

35. **C**

$$4130\left(4130\frac{6\%-4\%}{100}\times\frac{60}{365}\right)=4144$$

Remember, the convention we use for sterling products is to *pro rata* the year by Actual/365 days. Had this example been using a dollar product, then we would assume that every month has 30 days and a year has 360 days

See Chapter 3, Section 1.3 of your Study Text

36. **B** Gilt options are settled into futures rather than physically. The call is the right to buy, so if the holder exercises, they will buy/long the long gilt future

See Chapter 1, Section 1.17 of your Study Text

37. **C** All other payments will have been subject to variation margin, so you cash settle the final variation margin

See Chapter 1, Section 1.6.1 of your Study Text

38. **C** Neither party needs report as it is done automatically from the electronic trading system

See Chapter 3, Section 3.1.1 of your Study Text

39. **B** A buy limit order would be entered below the market, to close out and take profits. A buy stop order would be entered above the market to reduce losses on this position

See Chapter 3, Section 4.2.2 of your Study Text

40. **B** He should pay floating and receive fixed. Swap convention is that the pay side is quoted first

See Chapter 4, Section 1.4 of your Study Text

41. **A** Current portfolio has a delta of −4 (10 × 0.4), therefore buy 4 futures to achieve delta neutrality

Current = −4

Long futures = +4

Total = 0

See Chapter 3, Section 2.10 of your Study Text

42. **D** The long call at 740 will have an intrinsic value of 26p. The long put will have no intrinsic value

See Chapter 6, Sections 3.7.2 of your Study Text

43.   C   A putable bond has a feature that enables the holder to demand the issuer to repurchase the security

See Chapter 4, Section 4.4 of your Study Text

44.   C   The Over-the-Counter (OTC) market is more flexible as contract terms can be flexed to whatever the two counterparties agree. This will provide a more accurate hedging tool as the OTC derivative can be tailored to the exact risk of the client

See Chapter 1, Section 3 of your Study Text

45.   C   The at-the-money option will have the highest time value assuming they all have the same expiry. Since the underlying asset is trading at the same price as the strike, there is the greatest uncertainty as to whether the option will be exercised. This increased risk or uncertainty is reflected in the higher time value

See Chapter 3, Section 2.2 of your Study Text

46.   C   Specific terms of each deal are included in a confirmation

See Chapter 4, Section 2.1 of your Study Text

47.   C   The STIR futures and FRAs will provide a complete hedge. The interest rate cap will provide partial hedge to interest rate exposure. The S&P 500 future is based on US equities

See Chapter 6, Sections 3.10 and 4.2, and Chapter 5, Sections 1.2 and 1.3 of your Study Text

48.   C   This act now legalises the trading in single-stock futures and makes OTC derivative contracts legally enforceable

See Chapter 7, Section 2.3 of your Study Text

49.   B   Hitting the trigger level would require the customer to top up their maintenance margin to the initial margin level

See Chapter 5, Section 2.1.2 of your Study Text

50.   A   Gamma reflects not only the movement in the underlying but Delta (the change in premium for a given change in the underlying) moving relative to the underlying too

See Chapter 3, Section 2.11.1 of your Study Text

51.   B   Note that you must identify the answer that explains the difference between initial and variation margin. The key difference is that initial margin can be paid in collateral whereas variation margin must be paid in cash. Although the LME is an exemption to this rule, answer B is still the best available answer

See Chapter 5, Section 2.3 of your Study Text

52.   A   A credit derivative protects against a credit downgrade by allowing an investor to sell a bond at a pre-agreed price to the counterparty in the transaction

See Chapter 4, Section 1.9 of your Study Text

53. **C** GD means good for that day only. Sell MIT is entered above market, hence if market opens at 93.00, the trigger has not yet been reached. Once triggered, it would become a market order and could be filled at any price

   See Chapter 3, Section 4.2.6 of your Study Text

54. **D** This shows the put/call parity theorem in action! The purchase of a call and sale of a put with the same strike and same expiry will give a net result of a synthetic long future

   See Chapter 6, Section 3.2 of your Study Text

55. **D** Swap durations must be 5, 10 or 30 years

   See Chapter 4, Section 6.2 of your Study Text

56. **B** Deriv/SERV provides matching for OTC derivatives

   See Chapter 4, Section 6.3 of your Study Text

57. **B** The swaption is simply an option on a swap

   See Chapter 4, Section 1.4 of your Study Text

58. **B** You need to learn the specific responsibilities of the SEC and CFTC in the US for this exam

   See Chapter 7, Section 2.2 of your Study Text

59. **D** There are standardised contracts on several products trading on CME and SGX

   See Chapter 2, Section 3.2 of your Study Text

60. **B** A contango market is a normal market, meaning that the far-dated futures will be more expensive than the near-dated futures as the total cost of carry increases

   See Chapter 3, Section 1.4 of your Study Text

61. **B** The price of a FTSE 100 index option is quoted in index points and half index points. The tick is half an index point and the tick value is £5. Hence, the value of the FTSE 100 index option can be described as £5 per tick, £5 per half index point, or £10 per index point

   See Chapter 6, Section 5.3 of your Study Text

62. **B** Premiums are paid upfront for equity options on NYSE Liffe. This is defined as the business day following the day of trade

   See Chapter 3, Section 2.12 of your Study Text

63. **A** Although in certain circumstances all the other possibilities could be profitable if the interest rate spread changed, a basis swap is a swap specifically involving two floating rates of interest, which could relate to different currencies

   See Chapter 4, Section 1.4.2 of your Study Text

64. **C** Euro strengthening, yen weakening, therefore buy euro and sell yen. This you could undertake on the CME

   See Chapter 6, Section 2.2 of your Study Text

65.   **C**   The trade created is a horizontal spread, as it consists of buying and selling the same option strike but with different expiries. As the options have the same exercise price and are on the same underlying asset, their intrinsic value will always be the same. Therefore, the investor hopes to exploit an expected change in the relative difference between their time values

See Chapter 6, Section 3.11 of your Study Text

66.   **C**   The forward rate agreement (FRA) is the OTC equivalent. IRS stands for interest rate swap

See Chapter 4, Section 1.2 and Chapter 8, Section 4.2 of your Study Text

67.   **B**   The position created is a short strangle. The breakeven points will be upper strike plus both premiums, and the lower strike minus both premiums

See Chapter 6, Section 3.7.6 of your Study Text

68.   **C**   Hedgers are trying to protect themselves against future adverse price movements

See Chapter 1, Section 1 of your Study Text

69.   **A**   FRN is a Floating Rate Note, a type of bond. CMS – Constant Maturity Swaps, ARS – Average Rate Swaps and OIS – Overnight Index Swaps are all discussed in Chapter 5

See Chapter 4, Sections 3.3 and 3.4 of your Study Text

70.   **B**   Profit or loss = Ticks moved × Tick Value × No. of contracts

= 75 × £10 × 5

= £3,750

See Chapter 6, Section 1.3 of your Study Text

71.   **D**   It is more applicable to client-based services

See Chapter 7, Sections 1.1 and 1.2 of your Study Text

72.   **B**   In open outcry, exchange staff called Pit Observers relay the prices which are being transacted on the exchange floor which are then disseminated to the market

See Chapter 3, Section 3.1.2 of your Study Text

73.   **B**   The term backwardation implies that we do not normally expect to find the price for future delivery to be below today's cash price. This will arise when the asset yield exceeds the cost of carry. This means that investors would rather have the asset now and earn this high yield rather than receive delivery of the asset sometime in the future

See Chapter 3, Section 1.4 of your Study Text

74.   **C**   Fix the price of euros today as the US importer will have to buy €10m in one month's time. i.e. the importer is short euros. To hedge a short underlying position he enters into a long hedge

See Chapter 6, Section 3.9 of your Study Text

75.   **C**   The term GTC means good 'til cancelled, so the broker will continue to try and fill the order until they hear otherwise from the client

See Chapter 3, Section 4.2.11 of your Study Text

Practice Examination 3

75 Questions in 1 hour 30 minutes

1.   **How would you create a covered put?**

    A   Short position in asset/future and sale of put

    B   Long position in asset/future and sale of call

    C   Short position in asset/future and purchase of call

    D   Long position in asset/future and purchase of put

2.   **What would be the fair value of a 183-day S&P 500 future if the underlying index is trading at 8000, the dividend yield is 2.5% and the finance charge is 2%?**

    A   8081

    B   8102

    C   8163

    D   7980

3.   **Which of the following is the best definition of a future?**

    A   An obligation to buy a given quantity of an asset on a range of future dates at a predetermined price

    B   An agreement to buy or sell a standard quantity of a specified asset on a fixed future date at a price agreed today

    C   An agreement to buy or sell a standard quantity of a specified asset on a fixed future date at a price agreed in the future

    D   The right to buy or sell a standard quantity of a specified asset on a fixed future date at a price agreed today

4.   **Which trade is depicted below?**

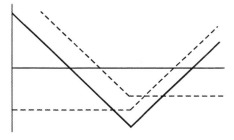

    A   Long strangle

    B   Short strangle

    C   Long straddle

    D   Short straddle

5. What is tick value?

      I   The product of multiplying tick size by contract size

      II   The profit or loss caused by a one-tick movement in price on one futures contract

      III   The smallest permitted price movement in a futures contract

      IV   A value used to calculated profit or loss on option trades which is dependent on the strike price of the option

   A   I only

   B   I and II

   C   III only

   D   I, II and IV

6. LCH.Clearnet operates which type of guarantee structure?

   A   Government-backed

   B   Independent

   C   Mutual

   D   Segregated

7. You sell two FTSE futures at 5000 at 10:00. The closing price at the end of the day on the future is 5053. If the initial margin is £3,000 per contract, and each point in the index represents £10, what is the total margin payment due to be made to LCH.Clearnet by 09:00 the next business day?

   A   £2,470

   B   £3,530

   C   £7,060

   D   £4,940

8. A customer is long 25 FTSE futures at 4000. He wishes to place an order to protect himself against an adverse movement. Which of the following orders would he submit?

   A   Buy MIT

   B   Sell stop

   C   Sell MIT

   D   Buy stop

9. Under the Commodities Futures Modernization Act where can SSFs be traded?

   A   On a Designated Contract Market

   B   On a Recognised Derivatives Transaction Execution System

   C   Anywhere provided appropriate risk warnings are given

   D   On open outcry markets only

10. **Which two of the following explain why variation margin is not paid out on NYSE Liffe individual equity options?**

    I   The option premium is paid by the start of the business day following the day of trade

    II   Individual equities are not as volatile as the index itself

    III   The standard contract value does not change throughout the life of the option

    IV   There is no marking to market of individual equity option positions

  A III and IV

  B II and III

  C II and IV

  D I and IV

11. **Which of the following trade affirmation systems would be used for credit derivative transactions?**

  A Affirm Xpress

  B Deriv/SERV

  C SWIFT

  D Swaps Wire

12. **To secure exemption under CFTC Part 30, FSA members must**

    I   Join the NFA arbitration scheme

    II   Pay funds, the amount calculated in accordance with the size and business of the firm, into an Escrow account at the NFA to cover any potential legal liabilities

    III   Provide the CFTC directly with any relevant customer records

    IV   Send and receive back from customers the generic CTFC risk disclosures

  A II, III and IV

  B I, II, III and IV

  C I, III and IV

  D I and IV

13. **When would a speculator undertake a horizontal trade?**

  A In a rising market

  B In a falling market

  C To profit from a change in volatility

  D To profit from an arbitrage opportunity

14. **Which of the following is false concerning OTC derivative markets generally?**

  A Liquidity may be low when compared to equivalent exchange-traded instruments

  B There is a risk of counterparty default that does not exist on exchange-traded markets

  C Products traded have a standard contract specification leading to a standardised product

  D There are often no margin requirements

15. **Of the four option strategies below, which will normally give the investor the greatest adverse daily time decay effect in money terms?**

   A   Short-dated short strangle

   B   Long-dated bull spread

   C   Short-dated long straddle

   D   Short-dated bear spread

16. **Which of the following is true of the arbitrage channel?**

   A   This is the area either side of the fair value of the future within which arbitrage trading will take place

   B   Every market participant will have an identical arbitrage channel

   C   The arbitrage channel is caused by such things as bid/offer spreads, commissions and exchange fees

   D   Professional arbitrageurs do not have an arbitrage channel and can therefore exploit any divergence between fair value and actual futures price

17. **What is the best definition of an interest rate swap?**

   A   Exchanging a fixed rate for a floating rate of interest on a notional amount for a fixed period of time with the difference paid at the end of the period

   B   Exchanging a fixed rate for a floating rate of interest on a notional amount for a fixed period of time with the difference paid at the start of the period

   C   Exchanging a fixed rate for a floating rate of interest on a notional amount for a fixed period of time with the difference paid at several times during the period

   D   Exchanging a fixed rate for a floating rate of interest on a notional amount with the difference paid at the end of the period

18. **What is the name of the flexible open source software used for OTC derivatives communication?**

   A   SwML

   B   FpML

   C   TriOptima

   D   TriReduce

19. **A customer holds a BBB bond and purchases a credit derivative. What is his motivation?**

   A   To protect against a credit downgrade

   B   To lock in a fixed rate of interest

   C   To have the right to sell back the bond if interest rates fall

   D   To have the right to sell back the bond if interest rates rise

20. **The US yield curve is currently inverted. If you expect the yield curve to rotate anti-clockwise and flatten, which of the following trades would you undertake?**

   A   Buy US T-bond future

   B   Sell US T-bond futures

   C   Sell three-month Eurodollar futures/buy US T-bond futures

   D   Buy three-month Eurodollar futures/sell US T-bond futures

21. **On delivery of a Long Gilt Future who does the seller deliver to?**

   A   The Exchange

   B   LCH.Clearnet

   C   The long holder direct

   D   The CGO

22. **NYSE Liffe variation margin debits are due**

   A   At the end of the business day

   B   At expiry of the contract

   C   By 09:00 the next business day after the last mark to market

   D   Immediately

23. **A gilt fund manager has a holding of the cheapest-to-deliver gilt with a market value of £120m and nominal value of £125m. If the nominal amount of a gilt future is £100,000 and the price factor of the cheapest to deliver gilt is 1.134545, which of the following represents the best hedge for the manager?**

   A   Buy 1,361 gilt futures contracts

   B   Sell 1,361 gilt futures contracts

   C   Buy 1,418 gilt futures contracts

   D   Sell 1,418 gilt futures contracts

24. **A portfolio holding of eight long futures contracts, three at-the-money long put options and two at-the-money long call options where the options have the same contract size as the future would have a net delta position of**

   A   +7.5

   B   +8.5

   C   +7

   D   +8

25. **Which of the following is least likely to be traded over the counter?**

   A   Swap

   B   Swaption

   C   FRA

   D   STIR

26. **Which of the following is false of basis and basis risk?**

   A   Basis risk is the risk of a change in basis affecting the user of a future

   B   When basis becomes less negative or more positive, it is said to weaken

   C   Basis is the result of deducting futures price from cash price

   D   In an efficient market, basis equals the cost of carry

27. **Calculate the fair value of the FTSE 100 index future, given the following information.**

Cash FTSE	6198
Interest rate	7% p.a.
Dividend yield	4.3% p.a.
Days until expiry	111

   A   6198

   B   6279

   C   6330

   D   6249

28. **Which two of the following are examples of an intermarket spread?**

   I   Buy a FTSE 100 future and sell a Long Gilt future

   II   Buy a FTSE 100 June future and sell a FTSE 100 September future

   III   Buy a Brent Crude June future and sell a Natural Gas June future

   IV   Buy a Brent Crude June future and sell a Brent Crude June future

   A   I and III

   B   I and IV

   C   II and III

   D   II and IV

29. **Which of the following statements are true?**

   I   Writers of options have the right to abandon those options

   II   The premium on an option is another name for the initial margin payment

   III   A European style option gives the writer the right to exercise the option on its expiry date only

   IV   The seller of an option is another term for the holder of an option

   A   III only

   B   III and IV

   C   None of the above

   D   I and II

30. **Which of the following statements about forwards is false?**

A Forwards are similar to futures, except they trade in the OTC market

B Forwards are always marked to market daily

C Forwards do not operate in a cash-cleared market

D Forwards are available on currencies, commodities and equities

31. **The guarantee offered by LCH.Clearnet extends as far as**

A The clearing member

B The non-clearing member using the clearing member's services

C All trading members of the exchange, but not the non-trading members

D The customer

32. **What is the appropriate order of the following actions?**

A Execute, give-up, match, clear, register

B Execute, give-up, match, register, clear

C Execute, match, register, give-up, clear

D Execute, match, give-up, register, clear

33. **Which of the following is NOT a correct definition of delta?**

A The absolute change in the price of the option given a change in the price of the underlying

B The percent change in the price of the option for a 1% change in the price of the underlying

C The probability of an option expiring in the money

D The proportion of the underlying asset needed to hedge an option

34. **Which of the following is an example of a diagonal spread?**

A Long 80 April call and long 100 June put

B Short 40 July put and long 40 October put

C Long 120 December call and short 140 December call

D Short 220 September put and long 200 June put

35. **How does LCH.Clearnet determine the level of a member's contribution to the member default fund?**

A According to the financial weight of the member

B According to the volume of trades and initial margin requirements of the member

C According to the credit rating of the member

D According to the financial record of the member

36. **What is the difference between broker's margin and LCH.Clearnet margin?**

A Brokers calculate margin using maintenance margin, LCH.Clearnet uses the SPAN margining system

B LCH. Clearnet calculates initial margin using the risk free rate, brokers may use a different rate

C Brokers may charge their clients a higher or lower margin than that charged by LCH.Clearnet, depending on the creditworthiness of the client.

D Brokers operate a gross margin system with their clients, LCH.Clearnet operates a net margin system

37. **Which of the following statements is true of an FRA?**

A The principal is actually exchanged

B The buyer will benefit if interest rates fall

C The settlement amount is subject to discounting

D The period over which the FRA is held is called the calculation period

38. **Calculate the treasurer's net profit or loss on this position as a result of the hedge.**

A company is due to receive £5m in two months' time in settlement of an outstanding invoice, when it will then place the funds on deposit for three months. The company treasurer is concerned that interest rates will fall in the interim period and wishes to hedge against this risk. He therefore buys ten short sterling contracts expiring in two months' time at 89.75 when the bank deposit rate for the relevant period is 9.75%. When the cash is received two months later, the treasurer sells the ten contracts at 90.25 when bank deposit rates are 9.10%.

A £1,875 profit

B £375 loss

C £1,875 loss

D £3,750 profit

39. **If LCH.Clearnet works out margins using the net positions of the company, will the company have**

A A margin buffer

B A joint buffer with LCH.Clearnet

C Larger margin payments

D Smaller margin payments

40. **A covered short call makes money in which market condition?**

A Bearish

B Very bearish

C Volatile

D Bullish neutral

41. **Which one of the following is not a function of the TRS system?**

   A   Assignment

   B   Settlement

   C   Matching

   D   Allocation

42. **A company knows that in one month's time it will need to borrow € 10m for a period of six months. What interest rate risk does the company have, and how can the company hedge the risk?**

	RISK	ACTION
A	Interest rates rise	Buy FRA
B	Interest rates fall	Buy FRA
C	Interest rates rise	Sell FRA
D	Interest rates fall	Sell FRA

43. **A futures speculator might seek to enter a long position in the market at a level below the current market by entering which of the following orders?**

   A   Buy MIT

   B   Buy stop

   C   Sell MIT

   D   Sell stop

44. **What are FRA prices based on?**

   A   Spot rates

   B   Forward rates

   C   Forward/forward rates

   D   Forward/spot rates

45. **What investment pays out based on the difference between the yield on an asset and a benchmark yield?**

   A   A credit-linked note

   B   An overnight swap

   C   A credit spread option

   D   A marked to market swap

46. **Two clients trade FTSE 100 futures through their brokers to open their positions, one going long, the other short. If the futures price rises from the traded price by the end of the day, what will be the flow of variation margin occurring in relation to this trade the following day?**

    A   Long pays buyer's broker pays seller's broker pays short

    B   Long pays short

    C   Short pays Clearing House pays long

    D   Short pays seller's broker pays buyer's broker pays long

47. **A synthetic long position is constructed by**

    A   Buy call, sell put, same strike and expiry

    B   Sell call, buy put, same strike and expiry

    C   Buy future, sell call

    D   Buy future, buy put

48. **Open interest is best described as**

    A   The sum of all long positions less all short positions open for delivery

    B   The net segregated long positions

    C   The total of short open positions

    D   The sum of all long segregated and house positions open for delivery

49. **The current price for the FTSE future stands at 4820-4821. A buy limit order at 4822 may be filled at**

    I   4820

    II   4821

    III   4822

    IV   4823

    A   I and II

    B   III and IV

    C   III only

    D   I, II and III

50. **If a market suddenly becomes more volatile and there is a large price fluctuation, which of the following margin calls is most likely to be made by a clearing house?**

    A   Increased initial

    B   Intraday

    C   Maintenance

    D   Variation

51. **A trade has been made on behalf of a customer that was subsequently found to contain an error. In which ONE of the following circumstances may the error be corrected?**

    A   The error was a genuine error and only of immaterial size

    B   There is evidence it was a genuine error and correction would not disadvantage the customer

    C   There is evidence that correcting the error will benefit the client

    D   The error was a significant error reported to a pit official

52. **Which of the following are not cash settled?**

    A   Interest rate swaps

    B   Spread-betting contracts

    C   Individual stock options

    D   Universal stock futures

53. **Which of the following options is likely to have the greatest gamma?**

    A   In-the-money, long dated

    B   Out-of-the-money, short dated

    C   At-the-money, long dated

    D   At-the-money, short dated

54. **The SEC administers which two of the following?**

    I   CBOT

    II   CBOE

    III   Stock index options

    IV   Bond futures

    A   I and II

    B   II and IV

    C   II and III

    D   I and IV

55. **What is the monetary equivalent of a portfolio that comprises five FTSE 100 futures when the underlying index is 4800 and the future is trading at 4820?**

    A   £48,000

    B   £48,200

    C   £240,000

    D   £241,000

56. **Which of the following trades would lead to the investor being exposed to the lowest level of risk?**

   A   An investor believing that the price of a financial instrument will rise buys a call and sells a put at the current price

   B   An investor believing that the price of a telecom company will rise buys a future on the given company

   C   An investor simultaneously buys a FTSE 100 future and sells a FTSE 100 call option

   D   An investor holds a portfolio of FTSE 100 stocks and buys a FTSE 100 put option

57. **When does settlement of an FRA take place?**

   A   At the beginning of the future period

   B   At the end of the future period

   C   At maturity

   D   At the discretion of the option older

58. **The following implied repo rates are calculated for the following deliverable bonds. If the notional coupon is 6%, which of the bonds is cheapest to deliver?**

	Bond	Implied Repo Rate
Treasury	10%	7.07%
Conversion	8.5%	8.14%
Conversion	9%	6.04%
Exchequer	11%	5.72%

   A   Treasury 10%

   B   Conversion 8.5%

   C   Conversion 9%

   D   Exchequer 11%

59. **A company has raised finance by issuing a bond paying a fixed rate of interest. The company now thinks interest rates will decrease. What contract should they enter into?**

   A   Swap floating for fixed

   B   Swap fixed for floating

   C   Swap fixed for fixed

   D   Swap floating for floating

60. **Which of the following is not a determinant of the priority of transactions being matched on LIFFE CONNECT?**

A Price

B Time

C Order type

D Underlying product

61. **If a broker is unable to pay variation margin what happens?**

A He is given a fine by the Exchange

B The amount he has to pay is taken from initial margin

C He is required to cease trading

D The amount he has to pay is taken from the client margin account

62. **When do payments actually take place under a plain vanilla swap?**

A Reset date

B Effective date

C Termination date

D Payment date

63. **Which one of the following statements is true?**

A A futures contract does not incur obligations to buy or sell an asset

B A future is standardised

C A future requires delivery of an asset

D A long future is the equivalent of a long put/short call at the same exercise price

64. **Which of the following is true of basis, sometimes referred to as 'crude' basis?**

A It is always negative

B It is always positive

C It is linear

D It is non-linear

65. **An investor is short 1,000 BT shares and buys one BT call. What is his synthetic position?**

A Long call

B Long put

C Short call

D Short put

66. **When an order has matched on the LIFFE CONNECT central order book, which of the following statements concerning trade reporting is true?**

    A   The seller must trade report the full details to NYSE Liffe

    B   The buyer must trade report the full details to NYSE Liffe

    C   The market maker must trade report the full details to NYSE Liffe

    D   Neither party has to report as the order book trades are reported automatically to NYSE Liffe

67. **The publication of which of the following would not contribute to price transparency in an electronic market?**

    A   Open interest

    B   Bid and offer prices

    C   Depth of bid and offer

    D   Last automatically executed trade

68. **Which of the following best describes the system of margining used in the UK and the US?**

    A   UK gross, US net

    B   UK net, US gross

    C   UK gross, US gross

    D   UK net, US net

69. **Which of the following would be the main reason why an investor may wish to trade a derivative OTC?**

    A   They will pay a lower margin

    B   They will pay lower fees

    C   The product will offer greater flexibility

    D   There will be lower credit default risk

70. **A futures hedge position may not give full protection against adverse price movements because**

    A   The basis may change

    B   Cash prices and futures prices usually move in unison

    C   The various futures months do not trade at the same price

    D   Transportation costs vary from one area to another

71. **What would be the maximum loss on the following trade?**

    Buy 180 call at a premium of 12

    Buy 180 put at a premium of 7

    A   12

    B   7

    C   19

    D   Unlimited

72. **Which style of regulation does the FSA employ?**

    A   Principles based

    B   Rules based

    C   Statutory based

    D   Law based

73. **How would you synthetically create the position of a long put?**

    A   Long future and short call

    B   Short future and short put

    C   Short future and long call

    D   Long future and long put

74. **Which of the following is a characteristic of the LIFFE CONNECT trading system?**

    A   It is order driven

    B   It is quote driven

    C   It is driven by the bid-offer spread

    D   It operates between 08:15 and 17:15

75. **Non-US firms that wish to trade directly on US exchanges for US citizens may do so if they**

    A   Apply for Part 30 exemption

    B   Abide by Part 30

    C   Register with the NFA

    D   Advise the FSA

Answers

1. **A**   A covered put is defined as writing a put option (i.e. selling the right to sell) and also having a short position in the underlying asset. Writing a put gives you a potential obligation to buy the underlying asset. It is covered, therefore, if you actually need/require the underlying (i.e. a short position in the underlying)

   See Chapter 6, Section 8.1 of your Study Text

2. **D**   Fair value = Cash + Net cost of carry (i.e. Finance charge – Dividend yield)

   $$= 8000 + [8000 \times (2\% - 2.5\%) \times 183/360]$$

   $$= 8000 + (-20.333)$$

   $$= 7979.667$$

   See Chapter 3, Section 1.3 of your Study Text

3. **B**   When looking for the best definition of a future, you should ensure that the following specific terms are present. "An **agreement** to buy or sell a **standard quantity** of a **specified asset** on a **fixed future date** at a **price agreed today**"

   See Chapter 1, Section 1.1 of your Study Text

4. **C**   The computer-based exams are using graphs so you need to be able to recognise the profiles of all strategies

   See Chapter 6, Section 3.7.2 of your Study Text

5. **B**   A tick is the minimum price movement allowed by the exchange and the tick value is the impact one tick movement has on one contract, e.g. the tick for the Brent Crude oil future is 1 cent. The future is priced per one barrel of oil. Given that the future is for a standard quantity of 1,000 barrels of oil, every time the future price moves by 1 tick (1 cent) the value of the 1,000 barrels (one contract) moves by 1 cent × 1,000 barrels = $10

   Therefore, $10 is the **tick value**

   See Chapter 6, Section 1.3 of your Study Text

6. **C**   The LCH operates a mutual guarantee structure whereby when a member defaults, the clearing house will use the resources of that member followed by the resources of all other members

   See Chapter 5, Section 1.3 of your Study Text

7.   C

	£
Initial margin 2 × £3,000	6,000
Variation margin (5053 – 5000) × £10 × 2	1,060 loss
Total margin due	7,060

Whilst this is the correct figure for total margin (initial and variation), bear in mind that initial margin can be paid in cash or collateral and variation margin must be paid in cash. Therefore, they are never netted off together

See Chapter 5, Section 2 of your Study Text

8:     B   A stop is a protective order to close out an existing position and to protect against further losses. A long future would make losses if the price fell, and to close out, a sell order would need to be triggered. Therefore, a sell stop would be the appropriate order

See Chapter 3, Section 4.2.4 of your Study Text

9.   A   A designated contract market is the official CFTC term for a derivatives exchange in the US

See Chapter 7, Section 2.3 of your Study Text

10.   D   As the option premium on NYSE Liffe equity options are paid upfront, we do not need to margin the holders. Variation margins are not paid out to the holder by LCH.Clearnet on the equity options. Note, if the price moves against the seller then he will have to pay in variation margin

See Chapter 5, Section 2.5.1 of your Study Text

11.   A   Affrim Xpress is part of the Deriv/SERV service provided by DTCC

See Chapter 4, Section 6.3 of your Study Text

12.   D   The firm need only provide access to customer records to the CFTC. Other requirements for Part 30 exemption include agreeing to jurisdiction of US courts and an obligation to abide by FSA/RIE rules

See Chapter 7, Section 2.4.1 of your Study Text

13.   C   Horizontal spreads involve and selling options of the same type (i.e. calls or puts), same strike but different maturity dates. Like straddles and strangles they are a method of trading volatility

See Chapter 6, Section 3.11 of your Study Text

14.   C   Common features of the OTC market in derivatives are that products are bespoke (tailor-made for clients) and, as a result, less liquid. There is no Clearing House for OTC contracts and therefore greater risk of counterparty default and in general, they are more lightly regulated. Due to the flexibility to negotiate specific contract requirements, there is a great deal of product proliferation

See Chapter 1, Section 3 of your Study Text

15. **C** Time decay hurts the holder of options (long positions) and helps the writer. It decays more rapidly as an option approaches expiry, therefore having the greatest impact on short-dated options

See Chapter 3, Section 2.2 and Chapter 6, Section 3 of your Study Text

16. **C** When a future is trading above or below fair value, a possibility exists to gain a risk profit from a cash and carry or reverse cash and carry. This possibility exists if the relevant trade can be constructed for a lower cost than the profit available. These costs include spreads, commissions and other charges and this represents an investor's arbitrage channel that is potentially different for all market participants depending on the individual costs they face

See Chapter 3, Section 1.6 of your Study Text

17. **C** The swap will usually be recalculated every three or six months during the life of the swap to determine the difference between the agreed fixed rate and the variable rate of interest for the next three of six months

See Chapter 4, Section 1.4 of your Study Text

18. **B** FpML

See Chapter 4, Section 6.4 of your Study Text

19. **A** Credit derivatives are purely about credit risk and not interest rate risk

See Chapter 4, Section 1.9 of your Study Text

20. **D** Short-term interest rates will fall, therefore, quote price will rise [100 – interest rate], therefore buy the three-month Eurodollar future. Long-term interest rates will rise, therefore, US T-bond prices will fall and, therefore, sell US T-bond futures

See Chapter 6, Sections 4.1 and 4.2 of your Study Text

21. **B** LCH.Clearnet is the intermediary for delivery and has accounts at CREST to accept delivery

See Chapter 2, Section 3 of your Study Text

22. **C** NYSE Liffe trades are cleared by LCH.Clearnet. Margin payments are collected automatically from LCH.Clearnet members' accounts via the Protected Payment System by 09:00 the business day following the relevant daily loss/debit

See Chapter 5, Section 1.5 of your Study Text

23. **D** $\dfrac{\text{Nominal value of CTD}}{\text{Face value of future}} \times \text{Price factor of CTD}$

$\dfrac{\text{£125m}}{\text{£100,000}} \times 1.134545$

= 1,418 contracts sold

See Chapter 6, Section 4.1.3 of your Study Text

24. **A**

8 Long futures delta +1 =	+8	(bullish, so positive delta)
3 Long ATM put delta −0.5 =	−1.5	(bearish, so negative delta)
2 Long ATM calls delta +0.5 =	+1	(bullish, so positive delta)
	+7.5	

A further potential exam question may ask how you could bring this portfolio back to delta neutrality (i.e. net delta of 0). Since 7.5 short futures is not a possible trade, the best available answer here would be long 15 ATM puts (ATM delta = 0.5 and long put is negative delta)

See Chapter 3, Section 2.10 of your Study Text

25. **D**   A STIR is a standardised exchange traded contract. They trade on NYSE Liffe

See Chapter 2 Section 1 of your Study Text

26. **B**   Basis is the difference between the cash price and the futures price. Hence, in a contango market, basis will be negative. Basis risk is the risk that the cash and the futures price do not move exactly in line with one another. In basis terminology, if basis gets more negative, it is weakening and if it is getting more positive, it is strengthening. It is true to say that in efficient markets basis is equal to the cost of carry

See Chapter 3, Section 1.5 of your Study Text

27. **D**   Fair value = Cash price + Cost of carry

$$= 6198 + \left(6198 \times \frac{7\% - 4.3\%}{100} \times \frac{111}{365} \right)$$

$$= 6198 + 51$$

$$= 6249$$

See Chapter 3, Section 1.3 of your Study Text

28. **A**   The term 'intermarket' means between two different but related markets. Hence, we need to select the spread between equities and bonds together with the spread between gas and oil futures. Items II and IV are 'intramarket spreads' as they are within the same market

See Chapter 6, Section 2.2 of your Study Text

29. **C**   In an options contract, the writer has a potential obligation to buy or sell an asset and therefore has no choices. European style options do indeed give the right to exercise on expiry date only, however, this right belongs to the holder/buyer, not the writer/seller as suggested in this question

See Chapter 1, Section 1.9 of your Study Text

30. **B**   Forward are not necessarily marked to market daily. Note that the reference to a cash cleared market implies an exchange with matching payments

See Chapter 4, Section 1.1 of your Study Text

31. **A**   LCH.Clearnet guarantees the performance of the contract, but this guarantee only extends as far as the clearing member. Members must manage their own risk with their clients

See Chapter 5, Section 1.1 of your Study Text

32. **D** Trades are executed and then matched. Trades of non clearing members are then allocated to clearing members (give-up). They are then ready for registration at the clearing house. Novation takes place at registration and the trade may then clear and settle

See Chapter 3, Section 5 of your Study Text

33. **B** Delta is a ratio of absolute amounts not a percentage

See Chapter 3, Section 2.10 of your Study Text

34. **D** A diagonal spread is the purchase and sale of the same type of option (both calls or both puts) with different strikes and different expiries. Answer B is an example of a horizontal spread (different expiries only). Answer C is an example of a vertical spread (different strikes only)

See Chapter 6, Section 3.11 of your Study Text

35. **B** The actual calculation is fairly complex but the level of business of the member is a key determinant of the required contribution to the default fund

See Chapter 5, Section 1.3 of your Study Text

36. **B** LCH.Clearnet uses SPAN to calculate initial margin and a component of SPAN is the risk free rate. Brokers must charge at least the SPAN margin but may charge more. They are not obliged to use any particular model to calculate margin. Consequently they can use a rate different from the risk free rate, use gross or net margining systems and operate an in initial plus variation margin system or a maintenance margin system

See Chapter 5, Section 2.4 of your Study Text

37. **C** The settlement amount is subject to discounting

See Chapter 4, Section 1.2 of your Study Text

38. **C** On futures

No. of ticks × Tick value × No. of contracts

$50 \times £12.50 \times 10 =$ £6,250   profit

On deposit – interest lost

$£5m \times \dfrac{(9.75\% - 9.10\%)}{100} \times \dfrac{3}{12} =$ £8,125   loss

Net loss   £1,875   loss

See Chapter 6, Section 4.2 of your Study Text

39. **D** If LCH.Clearnet nets off margin, it means that the margin owed by the company for trades done on one of the LCH.Clearnet-cleared exchanges (ICE futures, LME and NYSE Liffe) will be netted off against any margin owed to the company and, hence, margin payments will be lower

See Chapter 5, Section 1.2 of your Study Text

40. **D** A covered short call means the call writer is also long the physical asset. Therefore, the overall position is a synthetic short put and, as a result, the position is considered to be bullish/neutral

See Chapter 6, Section 8.1 of your Study Text

41. **B** TRS is not a clearing system for settlement. The settlement is done through LCH.Clearnet via the CPS system

    See Chapter 3, Section 5.1 of your Study Text

42. **A** Interest rates rise as this will increase the company's borrowing cost

    See Chapter 4, Section 1.2 of your Study Text

43. **A** Market-If-Touched orders (MIT) are used to trigger a market order to enter the market in a particular contract. Below the current price, you would believe that the contract was relatively cheap and therefore use a Buy MIT order to open a long position if the price hits the specified level

    See Chapter 3, Section 4.2.6 of your Study Text

44. **C** Forward/forward rates. Note that a forward rate is a quoted forward rate, whereas a forward/forward rate is the fair value of the forward rate, using money market spot rates

    See Chapter 4, Section 1.2 of your Study Text

45. **C** A credit spread option pays out if the difference between the yield on an asset (e.g. a risky bond) and a government bond yield rises above a certain pre-determined level

    See Chapter 4, Section 3.1 of your Study Text

46. **D** As the underlying has risen, variation margin profits are payable to the Long position. As the clients have traded via brokers, it is assumed that they are not themselves clearing members. Therefore, the variation margin flows will move via the brokers and then centrally via the Clearing House

    See Chapter 5, Section 2 of your Study Text

47. **A** A good shortcut for identifying synthetic positions is to use a variation of the put/call parity formula. From put/call parity, we know that a long call and a short put give a synthetic long position. Let's assume that a long position is a positive figure and a short position is negative. We can therefore say that

    $C - P = S$

    Where C is the call option (positive and therefore long), P is the short position (negative and therefore short) and S is the position in the future/underlying (positive and therefore long).

    $C - P = S$ tells us that a long call and a short put give a synthetic long

    We can also rearrange $C - P = S$ to identify different synthetics

    For example, Short 1,000 shares and long one call can be identified thus

    $C - P = S$

    $C - S = P$

    i.e. a synthetic long put

    See Chapter 6, Section 3.2 of your Study Text

48. **C** Either all the open longs or all the open shorts. This is a cumulative figure since trading in the contract began

    See Chapter 1, Section 2.2.2 of your Study Text

49. **D** At or better (i.e. lower) than 4822

See Chapter 3, Section 4.2.2 of your Study Text

50. **B** If the market suddenly becomes more volatile, the losses of a clearing member may already exceed the normal initial margin. Therefore, the clearing house may ask for immediate payment of margin within that day, i.e. intraday margin

See Chapter 5, Section 2.1.1 of your Study Text

51. **B** The exchange may allow the error to be corrected in order that the client's interests are protected

See Chapter 3, Section 4.3.1 of your Study Text

52. **C** Individual stock options are physically settled and therefore exercise results in taking/making physical delivery of the standard quantity (usually 1,000) of the underlying shares. Universal stock futures on NYSE Liffe are mostly cash settled with some physically settled, but stock futures on MEFF are physically delivered

See Chapter 1, Section 1.16 of your Study Text

53. **D** Gamma is the change in delta of an option, given a change in the value of the underlying asset. It describes how quickly a position is becoming increasingly/decreasingly bullish or bearish. Gamma is zero for deeply out-of-the-money and deeply in-the-money options. It is greatest for at-the-money options close to expiry

See Chapter 3, Section 2.11.1 of your Study Text

54. **C** The Securities Exchange Commission (SEC) regulates stock options and stock index options and the Chicago Board Options Exchange (CBOE). All other exchange-traded derivatives are regulated by the Commodity Futures Trading Commission (CFTC)

See Chapter 7, Section 2.2 of your Study Text

55. **D** Future price × £10 per index point × No. of contracts

= 4820 × £10 × 5 = £241,000

See Chapter 6, Section 3.8 of your Study Text

56. **D** Option A is a synthetic long, Option B is a long future and Option C is a covered short call. All of these positions would be profitable if the price of the future or underlying were to rise, but would result in increasing levels of losses were the future or underlying price to fall. Option D would effectively create a synthetic long call, with an unlimited potential profit, but a maximum loss limited to the option premium

See Chapter 6, Section 3.2 of your Study Text

57. **A** At the beginning of the future period (note: the payment is discounted)

See Chapter 4, Section 1.2 of your Study Text

58. **B** The highest implied repo rate is the cheapest-to-deliver bond

See Chapter 6, Section 4.1.2 of your Study Text

59. **B** A poorly worded question which depends on your interpretation of answers A and B. We've gone for B taking the exam question exactly as it is written where you are currently paying fixed and would like to swap it into the expected lower floating rate

See Chapter 4, Section 3 of your Study Text

60. **D** Orders on LIFFE CONNECT are matched according to the price stated, the time of input and the type of order placed. For example, market orders are likely to be matched ahead of limit orders

See Chapter 2, Section 2.3 of your Study Text

61. **B** When a broker cannot meet a variation margin call LCH.Clearnet will first use his initial margin. In most cases this will be sufficient as the initial margin is calculated to meet the worst probable one day loss. It is assumed that the is a clearing member making variation margin payments direct to LCH.Clearnet

See Chapter 5, Section 2 of your Study Text

62. **D** Payment date

See Chapter 4, Section 1.4.1 of your Study Text

63. **B** A future contract is standardised to the contract specifications. Answer D is wrong because a long put and short call at the same exercise price is a synthetic short position

See Chapter 1, Section 1 of your Study Text

64. **D** Basis will normally be negative, but can be positive in a backwardation market. It is non-linear, i.e. the relationship between the cash price and the futures price will not be constant

See Chapter 3, Section 1.5.1 of your Study Text

65. **B** A good shortcut for identifying synthetic positions is to use a variation of the put/call parity formula. From put/call parity, we know that a long call and a short put give a synthetic long position. Let us assume that a long position is a positive figure and a short position is negative. We can therefore say that

$C - P = S$

Where C is the call option (positive and therefore long), P is the short position (negative and therefore short) and S is the position in the future/underlying (positive and therefore long).

$C - P = S$ tells us that a long call and a short put give a synthetic long

We can now rearrange $C - P = S$ to identify different synthetics

Short 1,000 shares and long one call can be identified thus

$C - P = S$

$C - S = P$

i.e. a synthetic long put

See Chapter 6, Section 3.2 of your Study Text

66. **D** Since the LIFFE CONNECT system is a fully automated trading facility, the system is able to meet the members' trade reporting obligations automatically

See Chapter 3, Section 3.1.1 of your Study Text

67. **A** The amount of open interest is an indication of future liquidity in this market but would not indicate the current market price

See Chapter 1, Section 2.2.2 of your Study Text

68. **B** The UK operates a net clearing system for all the main exchanges through LCH.Clearnet. In the US, trades are settled on a gross basis through each individual exchange's clearing house

See Chapter 5, Section 1.2 of your Study Text

69. **C** The main benefit OTC products offer is increased flexibility with respect to size, maturity, underlying, etc

See Chapter 4, Section 1 of your Study Text

70. **A** A hedger always runs basis risk, as the futures price may change at a different rate to the underlying asset position they are trying to hedge

See Chapter 3, Section 1.5 of your Study Text

71. **C** This is a long straddle and the maximum loss is when the share price is unchanged and both premiums are paid

See Chapter 6, Section 3.7.2 of your Study Text

72. **A** The FSA has moved away from a rules based approach

See Chapter 7, Section 1 of your Study Text

73. **C** Remember to use the formula C – P = S. Transposed this gives C – S = P. Hence we need a long call and a short future

See Chapter 6, Section 3.2 of your Study Text

74. **A** LIFFE CONNECT is the electronic trading system for NYSE Liffe and is an order-driven system for derivative trading

See Chapter 2, Section 2.3 of your Study Text

75. **C** Part 30 exemption is only required when trading for US citizens on non-US exchanges. The NFA is the National Futures Association, which is the self-regulating organisation for derivatives traders in the US

See Chapter 7, Section 2.4 of your Study Text

Practice Examination 4

100 Questions in 2 Hours

1. **Which of the following is an intermarket spread?**

   A   Buying a STIR and selling a long gilt future

   B   Buying a STIR and selling a Euribor future

   C   Selling a STIR and selling a Euribor future

   D   Selling a STIR and selling a long gilt future

2. **What conclusion can we draw if the dividend yield is greater than the finance cost?**

   A   The price of an index future is trading below the actual index

   B   The price of an index future is trading above the actual index

   C   There is a mispricing in the market

   D   The cost of carry is positive

3. **Which of these options can be exercised over a variety of days?**

         I   American

         II   European

         III   Bermudan

         IV   Asian

   A   I and II

   B   I and III

   C   I and IV

   D   II and IV

4. **Which system is used to enable market participants to report trades and assign them to the correct account?**

   A   LIFFE CONNECT

   B   TRS

   C   CPS

   D   Liffe Reporting System

5. **In terms of risk and reward what is the position of the holder of an option?**

   A   Upside known, downside unknown

   B   Upside unknown, downside unknown

   C   Upside known, downside known

   D   Upside unknown, downside known

6. A broker enters into a number of exchange traded derivatives contracts with a variety of counterparties. The broker is a subsidiary of a bank and borrows money from the bank to meet its margin payments. The broker then finds itself unable to meet further payments. Who has the responsibility for directly compensating the broker's counterparties?

    A   The bank

    B   The FSA

    C   The Clearing House

    D   The Financial Services Compensation Scheme

7. A company has issued a bond and is paying a fixed rate. It believes that interest rates will fall and wants to reduce its cost of borrowing. What is the best option for achieving this?

    A   Enter into a FX swap

    B   Enter into a fixed for floating swap

    C   Enter into a put option

    D   Enter into a floating for fixed swap

8. In terms of put/call parity theorem, if an investor believes that the price of the call option is lower than it should be what trades should he effect?

    A   Buy the call, buy the put and short the underlying

    B   Buy the call, sell the put and short the underlying

    C   Buy the call, buy the put and long the underlying

    D   Buy the call, sell the put and long the underlying

9. What trade does this payoff diagram represent?

    A   Long call

    B   Long put

    C   Short call

    D   Short put

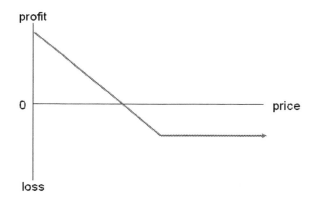

10. How is a synthetic short call created?

    A   Buy a put, buy the underlying

    B   Buy a put, sell the underlying

    C   Sell a put, sell the underlying

    D   Sell a put, buy the underlying

11. **What is spread margin?**

    A   A reduced form of margin that reflects offsetting trades

    B   Margin paid when spreads increase

    C   Margin paid at option expiry

    D   Maintenance margin

12. **A risk averse investor who is long a share believes that the price of the share will fall. What trade should he conduct?**

    A   A long call

    B   A short put

    C   A long put

    D   A short straddle

13. **All of the following statements are true, except**

    A   Exchange traded products are standardised

    B   The buyer and seller of an OTC product negotiate the terms

    C   The individual identity of the counterparty is known for an exchange traded product

    D   Exchanges offer greater liquidity

14. **An investor buys a share for 215p and buys a put option with a strike of 220p for 12p. The share price falls to 210p. What is the investor's profit or loss?**

    A   5p gain

    B   5p loss

    C   7p gain

    D   7p loss

15. **An investor buys 20 future and 10 call options with delta of 0.6. What is his position relative to the asset?**

    A   Long 14

    B   Short 14

    C   Long 26

    D   Short 26

16. **The FTSE is currently at 3800. Given that finance costs are 5% and the dividend yield is 2%, calculate the fair value of the future expiring in 29 days.**

    A   3809

    B   3815

    C   3792

    D   3785

17. **With respect to a forward rate agreement, what does the term '2v5' mean?**

   A   The FRA will start in 2 months time and end 5 months later

   B   The FRA will start in 2 months time and end 3 months later

   C   The FRA will start in 2 years time and end 5 years later

   D   The FRA will start in 2 years time and end 3 years later

18. **A bank has lent money to a company but is concerned about them going into liquidation. What is the best instrument to protect them against any loss?**

   A   A credit spread option

   B   A vanilla interest rate swap

   C   A currency swap

   D   A credit default swap

19. **A bank has in place an ISDA agreement with a counterparty. The counterparty subsequently goes into liquidation. What is the implication?**

   A   All contracts between the two parties are cancelled

   B   The contracts are netted and any money owed is paid by the bank to the liquidators or paid by the liquidator to the bank immediately

   C   The contracts are netted and the money owed is paid by the bank to the liquidators immediately or the bank, if owed money, becomes a general creditor

   D   The contracts are netted and the money owed is paid by the bank to the liquidators immediately or the bank, if owed money, writes off the money

20. **What is the definition of an amortising swap?**

   A   A swap whereby the notional amount rises over time

   B   A swap whereby the notional amount falls over time

   C   A swap whereby the notional amount falls and rises over time

   D   A swap such that the interest rate falls in predetermined steps over time

21. **What is the main purpose of regulation?**

   A   To protect the investor from financial crime

   B   To protect the investor from credit risk

   C   To protect the investor from counterparty risk

   D   To protect the investor from operational risk

22. **Which of these is true of gamma?**

   A   Gamma falls as the option approaches expiry

   B   Gamma moves in the same direction as delta

   C   Gamma will vary for options with different exercise prices

   D   It is a measure of implied volatility

23. When is the premium on a share option paid?

A   On the same day as the contract is traded

B   The day after the option is traded

C   On the expiry date of the option

D   When the option is closed out

24. Who initiates an assignment of an option?

A   The writer

B   The buyer

C   LCH

D   The exchange

25. With whom does LCH have a 'principal-to-principal' arrangement?

A   Brokers

B   Clients

C   Non-clearing members

D   Clearing members

26. An investor places an order to sell a future at a price below the current market price. He is willing to sell for this price but will accept a higher price. What type of order should he place?

A   Market order

B   Stop limit

C   Market if touched

D   Immediate or cancel

27. How long does a client have to cover unpaid variation margin?

A   One business day

B   Two business days

C   Three business days

D   Five business days

28. The holder of a short Long gilt future contract decides to make delivery. Which of these is true?

I   The long tells LCH which gilt he wants to receive

II   The short tells LCH which gilt he wants to deliver

III   The long tells LCH the day in the delivery month that he wants to take delivery

IV   The short tells LCH the day in the delivery month that he wants to make delivery

A   I and III

B   I and IV

C   II and III

D   II and IV

29. **Which of these options is out-of-the-money?**

      I   Call option, strike at 100, underlying at 110

      II   Call option, strike at 100, underlying at 95

      III   Put option, strike at 100, underlying at 110

      IV   Put option, strike at 100, underlying at 95

A   I and III

B   I and IV

C   II and III

D   II and IV

---

30. **Which of these would be used last in the event of default?**

A   Initial margin of the defaulting party

B   LCH profits

C   Insurance

D   Members Default Fund

---

31. **An investor has a holding of £20,000,000 of the CTD. Given that the contract size is £100,000 and the price factor is 1.0452116, what should the investor do to hedge this position?**

A   Buy 209 futures

B   Buy 191 futures

C   Sell 209 futures

D   Sell 191 futures

---

32. **Which of these is a diagonal spread?**

A   Sell FTSE June Call at 6000, Buy FTSE June Call at 6200

B   Sell FTSE June Call at 6000, Buy FTSE June Put at 6200

C   Sell FTSE June Call at 6000, Buy FTSE September Call at 6000

D   Sell FTSE June Call at 6000, Buy FTSE September Call at 6200

---

33. **What is the consequence for an authorised firm that 'treats customers fairly' and provides 'best execution'?**

A   Regulatory censure

B   Fall in profits

C   Good reputation

D   Criminal action

34. **A customer requires temporary assistance with margin payments from their broker. Where can the broker source the funding from?**

    A   The house account

    B   The client's margin at the clearing house

    C   Other segregated client accounts

    D   The firms own funds

35. **Why would an investor buy a receiver swaption?**

    A   To profit quickly if rates fall

    B   To protect against rates falling

    C   To profit quickly if rates rise

    D   To protect against rates rising

36. **An investor enters into an agreement to pay or receive the difference between two cash flows. One of the cash flows is related to a stock market index. What is the name for this type of agreement?**

    A   Basket switch

    B   Equity swap

    C   Interest rate swap

    D   Asset hedge

37. **Which body regulates exchanges in the UK?**

    A   Financial Services Authority

    B   Securities and Futures Commission

    C   Securities Exchange Board

    D   Monetary Authority

38. **Under International Accounting Standards, which of the following types of derivatives do not need to be shown at fair value?**

    A   Warrants

    B   Hedging instruments

    C   Out-of-the-money options

    D   Embedded options

39. **What is the main purpose behind the Financial Products Markup Language (FpML)?**

    A   To enable information regarding OTC transactions to be freely shared and transferred amongst all participants

    B   To reduce settlement costs and fees

    C   To enable the same information processing language as exchange traded derivatives

    D   To produce trading platforms

40. **With regard to OTC documentation, what is likely to be the impact of failing to clearly identify the local legal jurisdiction in which the trade has taken place?**

    A   The trade will not be legally enforceable

    B   The trade will not settle

    C   Interest payments will not be able to be calculated

    D   Margin requirements will not be met

41. **Which of the following is true regarding block trades?**

    A   The size of the deal does not need to be reported

    B   The price of the deal does not need to be reported

    C   It is the sole responsibility of the counterparty to check that prices and charges are fair

    D   The price may not be the same as the current market price

42. **A bank entering into a derivatives deal requests a haircut. How is this request met?**

    A   Extra collateral is posted above the value of margin required

    B   The deal is a no commission deal

    C   A special low interest rate applies

    D   Contracts can be voided by either party

43. **A fund manager with £500m of CTD bonds fears interest rates will rise. The CTD price factor is 0.73. What trade should he carry out to hedge?**

    A   Sell 3650 gilt futures

    B   Sell 3650 gilt options

    C   Buy 3650 gilt futures

    D   Buy 3650 gilt options

44. **Which of the following best describes the FSA's principal based regulation regime?**

    A   A set of detailed rules that must be complied with

    B   A set of high level general rules that must be complied with

    C   A set of high level rules that are voluntary in compliance

    D   A set of detailed rules which are voluntary in compliance

45. **How does an exchange cover its operational costs?**

    A   Exchange member fees and levies on all contracts

    B   Settlement fees and charges

    C   Through bid/offer spreads

    D   Through the member default fund

46. **When a Long Gilt future goes to delivery, how is it settled?**

    A   Physically between each party

    B   Through the BACS system

    C   Between members via CREST accounts

    D   Through LCH.Clearnet using CREST accounts

47. **What is the coupon of the notional bond in the contract specification for the NYSE Liffe long gilt future expiring in December 2007?**

    A   7%

    B   6%

    C   5%

    D   LIBOR + 1%

48. **A member of NYSE Liffe who only trades for himself using the CONNECT system is what type of member?**

    A   Remote

    B   General

    C   Individual

    D   Sole

49. **A put option has strikes available of 100 and 110. How would an investor create a bear put spread?**

    A   Buy the 100 strike and sell the 110 strike

    B   Buy the 100 strike and buy the 110 strike

    C   Sell the 100 strike and buy the 110 strike

    D   Sell the 100 strike and sell the 110 strike

50. **Which of these are TRUE of covered calls?**

        I   They are riskier than uncovered calls

        II   The are arbitrage trades

        III   They can be used to generate income

        IV   The writer of the call option will be long the asset

    A   I and II

    B   I and IV

    C   II and III

    D   III and IV

51. **The buyer of a Bermudan style payers swaption has the right to**

A   Enter a swap as the floating rate payer on set future dates

B   Enter a swap as the fixed rate payer on set future dates

C   Enter a swap as the fixed rate payer on expiration date only

D   Enter a swap as the floating rate payer on expiration date only

---

52. **What is the definition of fair value?**

A   The price of a future that makes it equivalent in economic value to the underlying asset

B   The difference between the price of a future and the price of the underlying asset

C   The same as the value of the basis

D   The future price in a contango market

---

53. **The seller of a FRA is the party that**

A   Makes a payment on the settlement date when the contract rate is higher than the settlement rate

B   Receives a payment on the settlement date when the contract rate is higher than the settlement rate

C   Makes a payment on the settlement date when the settlement rate is lower than the contract rate

D   Receives a payment on the settlement date when the contract rate is lower than the settlement rate

---

54. **The buyer of a Bermudan style receiver swaption is able to exercise**

A   On expiry date and enter in to a swap whereby they pay the fixed rate

B   On expiry date and enter in to a swap whereby they pay the floating rate

C   On a range of dates and enter in to a swap whereby they pay the floating rate

D   On a range of dates and enter in to a swap whereby they pay the fixed rate

---

55. **It is now May 15 and an investor believes that the price of ABC's shares is going to be stable in the next few months. What strategy would you recommend that he undertakes?**

A   Buy a call option on ABC with expiry in June

B   Sell a put option on ABC with expiry in June

C   Sell a straddle on ABC with expiry in June

D   Buy a strangle on ABC with expiry in June

56. **You buy a put option with a strike of 110p for 7p and sell a put option with a strike of 100p for 3p. Both options are over the same underlying with the same expiry date. What is the maximum profit per share?**

   A   3p

   B   4p

   C   6p

   D   10p

57. **Why would you undertake a horizontal spread?**

   A   Believe prices are going to rise

   B   Believe prices are going to fall

   C   Believe volatility is going to fall

   D   Believe prices are going to remain static

58. **What is the name of the system designed by LCH.Clearnet to enable OTC inter-bank swap market participants the ability to free up credit lines?**

   A   Repoclear

   B   Swapclear

   C   Derivs/SERV

   D   TriOptima

59. **The CTFC Part 30 allows**

   A   Trading in futures and options by all US investors through US dealers on all US exchanges

   B   Trading in futures and options by all US investors through US dealers on all non-US exchanges

   C   Trading in futures and options by all non-US investors through US dealers on all non-US exchanges

   D   Trading in futures and options by all non-US investors through non-US dealers on all non-US exchanges

60. **An investor is bearish on the LSE market but believes that shares in ABC represent good value. What should the investor do?**

   A   Buy the FTSE future and buy shares in ABC

   B   Buy the FTSE future and sell shares in ABC

   C   Sell the FTSE future and buy shares in ABC

   D   Sell the FTSE future and sell shares in ABC

61.	**A quote driven market is such that**

A	Market makers, intermediaries and inter dealer brokers display prices at which they are willing to trade

B	All market participants display prices at which they are willing to trade

C	Market makers, intermediaries and inter dealer brokers display prices and volumes at which they are willing to trade

D	All market participants display prices and volumes at which they are willing to trade

62.	**Which of these will not affect the speed with which an order will be executed?**

A	Price

B	Time

C	Order type (e.g. limit order, market order)

D	Security

63.	**The mutual offset system allows for a trade executed on one exchange to be closed out on another. Between what exchanges is this facility available?**

A	CME and Eurex

B	CME and SGX

C	CME and NYSE Liffe

D	CME and Osaka

64.	**Which is TRUE of options on futures?**

A	The underlying is a futures contract

B	The premium is always paid on close

C	Unlike other options the buyer is always margined

D	They only trade on NYSE Liffe in the UK

65.	**The process of cancelling a trade and replacing it with another or changing one of the parties to a trade is known as**

A	Nomination

B	Substitution

C	Allocation

D	Novation

66.	**A cross trade is a trade such that**

A	A firm buys from one of its clients as the counterparty to the trade

B	A firm sells to one of its clients from its own inventory

C	A firms buys from one of its own clients and sell to another of its clients at the same time

D	A firm executes a client trade through an inter-dealer broker

67. **Orders placed by two investment banks are matched on LIFFE CONNECT. Which party has the responsibility for reporting the trade?**

    A The selling party

    B The buying party

    C Both parties must report

    D Neither party

68. **Which of these circumstances is likely to lead to an intra-day margin call on a share option?**

    A The share is about to pay a dividend

    B Unexpected volatility in the share price

    C A contract nears its expectation date

    D The open interest increases

69. **An investor pays an initial margin of £10,000 and sets a margin top-up limit of £8,000. The margin account reaches £7,750. Which of the following is true?**

    A The broker must close out the client's position immediately

    B The client must pay in £250 or have the position closed out

    C The client must pay in £2,250 or have the position closed out

    D The client must pay 20% of the initial margin

70. **An investor sells a near dated 500p call option for 25p and buys a far dated 575p call option for 34p. What type of spread is he selling?**

    A Vertical spread

    B Bull spread

    C Horizontal spread

    D Diagonal spread

71. **A holder of a credit default swap could exercise his rights in which of the following circumstances?**

    A When the credit is downgraded

    B In the event of a liquidity squeeze in the market

    C After an interest rate increase

    D At a restructuring of the company's debt

72. **At what points will an investor break even if he sells a 100p call for 4p and sells a 100p put for 8p?**

    A 88p and 112p

    B 92p and 108p

    C 96p amd 104p

    D 100p and 100p

73.   What is the fair value of the following 183 day future if the underlying trades at $800, the financing costs are 2% and the coupon is 2.5%?

A $796

B $798

C $802

D $804

74.   An investor receives a call from his broker stating that additional margin is required due to an increase in volatility. What is the name of this type of margin?

A   Spot margin

B   Initial margin

C   Intra day margin

D   Variation margin

75.   Which of the following is a calendar spread?

A   Buy a May 100 call and sell a June 110 call

B   Buy a May 100 call and sell a June 100 call

C   Buy a May 100 call and sell a May 110 call

D   Sell a May 90 put and buy a May 100 put

Answers

1. **A** An intermarket spread is one where futures positions are bought in one delivery month and sold in the same delivery month but in a different but related contract

   See Chapter 6, Section 2.2 of your Study Text

2. **A** The cost of carry = Finance cost – Dividend yield = A negative value

   The price of the future thus must be below the cash price

   See Chapter 3, Section 1.3 of your Study Text

3. **B** American can be exercised anytime between the trade date and the expiry date. Bermudan options will have a series of days/periods during which they can be exercised

   See Chapter 4, Section 5 of your Study Text

4. **B** The exchange's Trade Registration System is used to perform these functions. LIFFE CONNECT is NYSE Liffe's trading system and CPS is the Clearing and Processing System operated by LCH.Clearnet

   Note: Liffe reporting system is fictitious

   See Chapter 3, Section 5.1 of your Study Text

5. **D** The buyer (holder) of an option cannot lose more than the premium which is known beforehand. The upside is dependent on market performance

   See Chapter 1, Sections 1.11 and 1.13 of your Study Text

6. **C** LCH.Clearnet acts as counterparty to each clearing member once the trade has been novated. Hence, LCH.Clearnet assumes direct responsibility. Remember, once novation has occurred the original parties to the trade have no relationship whatsoever

   See Chapter 5, Section 1.2 of your Study Text

7. **D** Here you want to pay floating and receive fixed to benefit from falling interest rates

   See Chapter 4, Section 1.4 of your Study Text

8. **B** The starting point for this question is to recall the equation $C – P = S$

   We notice that the call option is lower than expected so we buy it. The above equation tells us that if we buy the call then we should sell the put. The effect is to create a synthetic long. To benefit from the price correction that will occur in the market we should sell the underlying

   See Chapter 3, Section 2.7 of your Study Text

9. **B** This is the payoff diagram for a long put. The examiner is using diagrams more frequently in the exam. It is important that you learn them

   See Chapter 1, Section 1.13 of your Study Text

10. **C** Again the starting point here is to consider the equation $C - P = S$

We then re-arrange to get $C = S + P$ and finally multiply all the terms by -1 to get $-C = -S - P$

This then tell us that to create a synthetic short call, i.e. $-C$, we sell the underlying ($-S$) and sell the Put ($-P$)

See Chapter 6, Section 3.2 of your Study Text

11. **A** An example would be the margin required when you enter into a vertical spread. The maximum loss using this strategy is capped even though you are selling an option. It might even be that there is no margin to pay, e.g. when the premium that you pay on one leg is greater than the premium that you receive on the other

See Chapter 5, Section 2.6.3 of your Study Text

12. **C** A short straddle would be an effective strategy if the share price dropped by a limited amount. However, we are told here that the investor is risk adverse so he would not want to face the risk of the market dropping by a large amount. A long put would protect against a large fall in share price

See Chapter 6, Section 5.2 of your Study Text

13. **C** Exchange traded products are normally novated through the clearing house or the exchange. This means that the buyer has a contract directly with the clearing house and the seller has a separate contract directly with the clearing house, such that the buyer and seller remain anonymous to each other

See Chapter 2, Section 3 of your Study Text

14. **D** Money out = 215p (to buy the share) + 12p (to buy the option) = 227p

Money in = 220p (sale of share using the option)

Loss = 7p

See Chapter 1, Section 1.13 of your Study Text

15. **C** The two trades are bullish hence the deltas are positive

Net delta = 20 + (10 × 0.6) = 20 + 6 = +26

See Chapter 3, Section 2.10 of your Study Text

16. **A** Future price = Cash price + Cost of carry

= 3800 + (3800 × (5% - 2%) x 29/365)

= 3800 + 9

= 3809

See Chapter 3, Section 1.3 of your Study Text

17. **B** This sort of question is often asked. The first number tells you when it starts and the difference in the numbers tells you how long it lasts for

Note: don't confuse months and years

See Chapter 4, Section 1.2 of your Study Text

18. **D** Clearly the answer is either a credit spread option or a credit default swap. The option is really used to provide compensation in the event of a downgrading whereas the swap protects against a failure to pay, i.e. default/liquidation

See Chapter 4, Sections 1.9 and 3.1 of your Study Text

19. **C** Without an ISDA agreement the bank would have to pay the gross amount owing on its contracts and would become a general creditor for all money owed to it

See Chapter 4, Section 2.1 of your Study Text

20. **B** Make sure that you learn about the different types of swaps. The examiner also often asks about accreting (where the notional rises over time) and rollercoaster (where the notional falls and rises over time)

See Chapter 4, Section 3.4.1 of your Study Text

21. **A** Given that Market Confidence and Reducing Financial Crime are stated FSA objectives this is the best answer. Operational risk is managed by having in place sufficient capital (as required by the Capital Requirements Directive) and robust processes and procedures. Counterparty risk is very much part of credit risk is managed by doing credit checks, credit lines and processes such as margining, netting and DVP settlement

See Chapter 7, Section 1 of your Study Text

22. **C** Gamma will be greatest for at-the-money options and will thus reduce for options in-the-money and out-the-money

See Chapter 3, Section 2.11.1 of your Study Text

23. **B** Premium for options on shares, the FTSE and options on LME futures are paid upfront. This actually means by 09:00 the next morning using LCH's Protected Payment System

See Chapter 5, Section 2.5.1 of your Study Text

24. **B** The key word here is 'initiates'. It is only if the buyer/holder chooses to exercise that assignment will occur

See Chapter 3, Section 5.2 of your Study Text

25. **D** LCH.Clearnet only offer this to Clearing Members

See Chapter 5, Section 1.2 of your Study Text

26. **B** A market order will execute immediately at the current market price. Market-if-touched will only become active once the stated price is reached in the market but faces risk in that the order then becomes a market order and could execute below the stated price. Immediate or cancel will happen, or not, immediately

See Chapter 3, Section 4.2.5 of your Study Text

27. **D** The broker is allowed to cover margin for five days only

See Chapter 5, Section 3.2 of your Study Text

28. **D** Whilst option holders have choices, it is the seller of the future who has the ability to make choices. This will mean that they will do what is best for them which obviously means not best for the buyer

   See Chapter 6 Section 4.1 of your Study Text

29. **C** Options are out-of-the-money if there is no intrinsic value

   See Chapter 3, Section 2.1 of your Study Text

30. **C** The insurance is provided by AAA-rated US insurers but it is very much a last resort. It is important to learn the list of available resources and order used

   See Chapter 4, Section 1.9 of your Study Text

31. **C** Again the starting point for this type of question is to establish whether the investor should buy or sell futures. A long position is protected using a short hedge, i.e. selling futures. Thus we can narrow the answer down to a choice from two

   $$\text{The number to sell} = \frac{\text{Nominal value of CTD bond held}}{\text{Face value of the future}} \times \text{Price factor of CTD}$$

   = 1.00452116 = 209

   $$\frac{20,000,000}{100,000}$$

   See Chapter 6, Section 4.1.2 of your Study Text

32. **D** A diagonal spread involves buying and selling calls with different expiry dates and different strikes

   See Chapter 6, Section 3.11 of your Study Text

33. **C** Firms that act in this way will please the FSA and its customers

   See Chapter 7, Section 1.2 of your Study Text

34. **D** The firm is not allowed to use client money so we are left with two choices. The house account will be margined against LCH so those funds are unavailable. Thus the firm will have to use its own funds

   See Chapter 5, Section 3.2 of your Study Text

35. **B** A receiver swaption would be used by a depositor receiving a floating rate who is concerned about rates falling. If rates fall and he has bought a receiver swaption , he will be able to exercise his option and will then receive fixed and pay floating. Effectively he can create a floor in terms of what he receives. If rates rise he can continue to receive floating and potentially abandon his option. To profit quickly if rates fall he could enter into an interest rate swap whereby he pay floating and receives fixed

   See Chapter 4, Section 1.4.2 of your Study Text

36. **B** An equity swap involves swapping the return on an index for a referenced interest rate

   See Chapter 4, Section 1.6 of your Study Text

37.　**A**　The regulator in the UK is called the Financial Services Authority

See Chapter 7, Section 1 of your Study Text

38.　**B**　Derivatives must be recognise at fair value on the balance sheet unless they are used for hedging

See Chapter 7, Section 4.3 of your Study Text

39.　**A**　Available free of charge, FPML's purpose is to automate the flow of information across the derivatives network. Basically it enables systems to communicate with each other

See Chapter 4, Section 6.4 of your Study Text

40.　**A**　It is essential that firms identify if an ISDA agreement is enforceable in the local jurisdiction

See Chapter 4, Section 2.1 of your Study Text

41.　**D**　Block trades are done away from LIFFE CONNECT so the price may not be the same as the current market price

See Chapter 1, Section 3.1.1 of your Study Text

42.　**A**　A haircut is the word used to describe the excess value of stock that is required to cover a cash exposure. For example, if you lend another party £1,000,000 in cash and accept £1,000,000 of stock as collateral you are exposed in that the value of the stock can fall quickly in the market. To protect against this you might request £1,100,000 in stock. This will mean that the stock will have to fall by £100,000 in value before you are exposed

See Chapter 5, Section 3.1 of your Study Text

43.　**A**　$\dfrac{500,000,000}{100,000} \times 0.73$

Therefore sell 3650 futures

See Chapter 6, Section 4.1.3 of your Study Text

44.　**B**　Whilst the use of the word 'principles' might be better here than the word 'rules' the basic premise is that the requirements are high level and must be complied with

See Chapter 7, Section 1.2 of your Study Text

45.　**A**　The key word here is 'exchanges'. Settlement fees and charges are levied by depositories such as Euroclear UK and Ireland. Bid/offer spreads are used by market makers and the member default fund is used by LCH.Clearnet to protect itself and the markets

See Chapter 3, Section 1 of your Study Text

46.　**D**　Intervention in the settlement of a future is a key role of LCH.Clearnet. Remember trading on LIFFE CONNECT is anonymous and once a trade is novated the two original parties to the trade have no relationship. If the exchange of securities and cash was between members then, to a certain extent, it defeats the purpose of anonymity

See Chapter 5, Sections 1.4 and 1.6 of your Study Text

47. **B** You are expected to know the full details of the contract specification for the main NYSE Liffe products. The long gilt future has a notional coupon of 6% and a nominal value of £100,000

See Chapter 6, Section 4.1.1 of your Study Text

48. **C** This describes individual members

See Chapter 5, Section 1.1 of your Study Text

49. **C** Spreads are constructed by buying one contract and selling another. Remember for BULL spreads we Long the Low. Thus for BEAR spreads we must Long the High

See Chapter 6, Section 3.3 of your Study Text

50. **D** The phrase 'covered calls' tells us immediately that the writer of the option is covered, i.e. he holds the asset. Clearly if an investor is selling options he is raising cash and therefore generating revenue. Note: this strategy might be employed by an asset manager who believes that the market is going to be static

See Chapter 6, Section 8.1 of your Study Text

51. **B** Remember that the buyer of a payers swaption pays fixed. Bermudan style is somewhere between American style and European style, i.e. you can't exercise everyday and you are not restricted to exercising on expiry date. Instead there will be a variety of day/periods when you can exercise

See Chapter 4, Sections 1.4 and 5 of your Study Text

52. **A** Fair value is calculated by adding on the cost of carry to the cash price. Of course, cost of carry could be a negative value

See Chapter 3, Section 1.2 of your Study Text

53. **B** With an FRA, the buyer pays fixed and the seller receives fixed. Note: the contract rate is the fixed rate and the settlement rate is the floating rate at the time of settlement. The seller of an FRA will, therefore, receive a payment if the contract rate (fixed rate) is greater than the settlement rate (floating rate)

See Chapter 4, Section 1.2 of your Study Text

54. **C** Bermudan style options have a variety of possible expiry dates. We are, therefore, drawn to the two answers that allow for a range of dates. The term 'receiver swaption' tells us that the buyer of the option will receive fixed and , therefore, pay floating

See Chapter 4, Sections 1.4 and 5 of your Study Text

55. **C** Certainly we are looking to sell options since we would only want to buy if we expected price movement. A straddle is the best choice since we can collect two premiums

See Chapter 6, Section 3.7.3 of your Study Text

56. **C** Here the maximum loss is 4p. The maximum profit is given by the difference in strikes (110 – 100 = 10p) minus the max loss

See Chapter 6, Section 3.3 of your Study Text

57. **C**   Horizontal spreads exploit a view on volatility. Therefore C is the best available answer

See Chapter 6, Section 3.1.1 of your Study Text

58. **B**   Repoclear is also a system developed by LCH. Derivs/SERV is a matching service provided by DTCC and TriOptima is specialised software for reducing down a portfolio of OTC trades into a smaller number

See Chapter 4, Section 6.2 of your Study Text

59. **A**   There is no mention of CFTC Part 30 exemptions in this question. We can rule out references to non-US exchanges since this is only allowed if the product has been approved by the CFTC

See Chapter 7, Section 2.4 of your Study Text

60. **C**   An obvious answer. The examiner does ask questions as simple as this. Don't look for complications when they don't exist

See Chapter 1, Section 1 of your Study Text

61. **C**   Only market professional display prices and volumes in an order driven market

See Chapter 2, Section 2.3 of your Study Text

62. **D**   Price and time affect the position that the trade takes on the order book. Clearly market orders will execute straight away whilst limit orders might have delayed execution

See Chapter 3, Section 4.2 of your Study Text

63. **B**   The mutual offset system allows trades conducted on CME to be closed out on SGX and vice versa

See Chapter 2, Section 3.2 of your Study Text

64. **A**   Options on futures exercise into futures positions

See Chapter 1, Section 1.17 of your Study Text

65. **D**   This is the definition of novation

See Chapter 2, Section 3 of your Study Text

66. **C**   The firm acts for both clients and offers them a price that is generally favourable to both. Note the firm cats as a broker here and makes money by charging both clients commission

See Chapter 3, Section 4.1 of your Study Text

67. **D**   For trades done on electronic systems reporting is done automatically so neither party has to report the trade

See Chapter 3, Section 3.1.1 of your Study Text

68.   **B**   The initial margin is calculated using the expected largest daily movement in the underlying asset price and is used to protect LCH against such a movement. The variation margin process is further designed such that at the start of the day, throughout the period during which a party has an open contract, LCH has sufficient protection to protect against a change in the value of the contract up to the initial margin level. Should the share display excessive volatility the cash held by LCH may not be sufficient to cover the daily loss on a contract. Thus, LCH will issue an intra-day margin call

See Chapter 6, Section 2.6.5 of your Study Text

69.   **C**   The wording of this question did not use the term 'maintenance margin' but 'top up' or 'margin limit'. However it seems to be referring to the maintenance margin system which operates in the US but can also be operated by the UK brokers with their clients. The trigger level of £8,000 or less remaining on the margin account requires the client to top the account back up to the £10,000 initial level

See Chapter 5, Section 2.1.2 of your Study Text

70.   **D**   A combination of long and short call, with different strikes and expiry dates is a diagonal spread

See Chapter 6, Section 3.11 of your Study Text

71.   **D**   If the reference asset or its creditors initiate debt restructuring this will change the status priority of the default swap and the buyer will receive payment

See Chapter 4, Section 1.9 of your Study Text

72.   **A**   This strategy is known as a short straddle. The breakeven points will therefore, be the strike plus total premium received and strike minus total premium received

See Chapter 6, Section 3.7.3 of your Study Text

73.   **B**   Fair value = Cash + Cost of carry

$800 + ($800 × (2.0% − 2.5%) × (183/360))

= $798

See Chapter 3, Section 1.3 of your Study Text

74.   **C**   Intra day margin is called when volatility in an underlying asset accelerates

See Chapter 5, Section 2.6.5 of your Study Text

75.   **B**   Buy a May 100 call and sell a June 110 call = Diagonal spread
Buy a May 100 call and sell a June 100 call = Horizontal/calendar spread
Buy a May 100 call and sell a May 110 call = Vertical bull spread (calls)
Sell a May 90 put and buy a May 100 put = Vertical bear spread (puts)

See Chapter 6, Section 3.11 of your Study Text

Practice Examination 5

100 Questions in 2 Hours

1. **Which of the following is the most accurate description of a seller of a futures contract?**

    A The seller of a future is under an obligation to sell a customised amount of a non-specified asset on a future date at a price determined in 3 months' time

    B The seller of a future is under an obligation to sell a standardised amount of a non-specified asset on a future date at a price determined in 3 months' time

    C The seller of a future is under an obligation to sell a standardised amount of a specified asset on a fixed date at a price determined in 3 months' time

    D The seller of a future is under an obligation to sell a standardised amount of a specific asset on a fixed date at a price agreed today

2. **A broker opens a position on CME and closes it on SGX. This is known as**

    A Futures exchange settlement system

    B Mutual offset

    C Net settlement

    D Intermarket spread

3. **A 100 strike call has a price of 70p and a delta of 0.87. What will be the impact on the price of the call option if the underlying rises by 5p?**

    A 4.35p

    B 3.7p

    C 2.85p

    D 1.65p

4. **What is the advantage of Exchange Price Feeds?**

    A To provide real time prices

    B To match trading parties

    C To allocate limit orders

    D To display clearing information

5. **When can a customer continue to open new contracts if they have used up all their available credit line with a dealer?**

    A When they have a high credit rating

    B When they post extra collateral to cover the payments required for the new business

    C They cannot continue to open new contracts

    D When they agree to post new collateral in good time after the deal

6. **Which of the following is an accurate characteristic of a forward contract?**

    A   A forward is standardized across asset classes

    B   A forward is traded on exchange

    C   A forward's delivery dates are predetermined by the exchange

    D   A forward can be customized by the counterparties

7. **A borrower concerned that interest rates are going to rise would most likely purchase which of the following OTC products?**

    A   A cap

    B   A floor

    C   A bear spread

    D   A bull spread

8. **An investor has bought an option that gives him the right but not the obligation to enter into an interest rate swap where he will be receiving a fixed rate in exchange for a floating rate. Which one of the following has he purchased?**

    A   A call option

    B   A receiver cap

    C   A receiver swaption

    D   A collared cap

9. **A broker has only two clients, A and B, and no positions of its own. A is long ten futures contracts and B is short ten contracts. Which of the following is false?**

    A   The broker has no positions with the clearing house

    B   The broker has no margin with the clearing house

    C   The clients must close out their positions to avoid delivery

    D   The clients both have margin with the broker

10. **Initial margin must be paid**

    A   Prior to opening the position

    B   Within 5 minutes of opening the position

    C   Within 15 minutes of opening the position

    D   By 09:00 the following day

11. **State the order in which the following processes will occur for the settlement of a future through LCH.Clearnet.**

    I   LCH.Clearnet will randomly match a buyer with a seller

    II   The seller announces to LCH.Clearnet that they wish to deliver under the contract

    III   LCH.Clearnet calculates the exchange delivery and settlement price

    IV   Settlement of the physical asset and exchange of the cash take place

  A   II, III, I, IV

  B   II, I, IV, III

  C   II, I, III, IV

  D   III, I, II, IV

12. **Which of the following clearing members can act for themselves and for their direct clients only?**

  A   General clearing members

  B   Associate clearing members

  C   Client clearing members

  D   Individual clearing members

13. **An equity fund manager wants to hedge a $30m portfolio that tracks the S&P 500. The S&P future is at 1425 and the contract is $500 an index point. How many futures are required for the hedge?**

  A   26,667

  B   0.02

  C   2.9

  D   42

14. **Which of the following is not one of the six TCF outcomes?**

  A   Fair treatment of customers is paramount

  B   Information provision is clear

  C   Consumers are protected from financial crime

  D   Consumer do not face unreasonable post sale barriers

15. **In the US, derivatives regulation is split between two government bodies. Which are they?**

  A   The SEC and FSA

  B   The SEC and CFTC

  C   The CFTC and FSA

  D   The FSA and MiFID

16. **An investor buys a call with a higher strike and a put with a lower strike what is his strategy called?**

    A   Bull spread

    B   Bear spread

    C   Long strangle

    D   Long straddle

17. **Which of the following must be authorised?**

    A   Futures and option funds

    B   Geared futures and option funds

    C   Both futures and option funds and geared futures and options funds

    D   Neither futures and option funds nor geared futures and options funds

18. **Which of the following is an advantage of using a derivatives account versus investing in a fund?**

    A   Greater diversification

    B   Structured product

    C   Lower cost

    D   Unlimited liability

19. **When determining whether a derivatives position should be included in calculations of stake size in merger and acquisition which of the following provides the most accurate description provided by the DTR rules?**

    A   A derivative is a financial product whose value is in whole determined directly by reference to the price of an underlying security

    B   A derivative is a financial product whose value is in part determined indirectly by reference to the price of an underlying security

    C   A derivative is a financial product whose value is in whole or in part determined indirectly by reference to the price of an underlying security

    D   A derivative is a financial product whose value is in whole or in part determined directly or indirectly by reference to the price of an underlying security

20. **The framework for accounting for derivatives at fair value is found in which of the following International Accounting Standards?**

    A   IAS 12

    B   IAS 24

    C   IAS 39

    D   IAS 42

21. **Basis will be higher when**

    A   There is strong demand in the cash market

    B   Interest rates are low

    C   The contract nears expiry

    D   There is low liquidity

22. **Which of the following would not be one of the inputs into the Black Scholes model when determining the implied volatility of an option?**

    A   Strike price

    B   Counterparty

    C   Time to expiry

    D   Market price of option

23. **An investor goes short 10 long gilt contracts. Initial margin will be**

    A   Reduced down against existing positions

    B   Reduced down by any unrealised profits on open positions

    C   Subject to a haircut, including cash collateral

    D   Payable in cash or collateral on the gross position

24. **If an investor buys a 100 strike call for 8 and sells a 106 strike call for 4 what is the maximum profit per share?**

    A   18

    B   10

    C   -4

    D   2

25. **Which two of the following trades create a synthetic short put?**

    A   Long equity and Long call

    B   Long equity and Short call

    C   Short equity and Long call

    D   Short equity and Short call

26. **An investor who has entered into a contract to purchase a specific amount of an underlying physical commodity from a seller in an off exchange transaction wishes to take his position on exchange. Which of the following transactions would correctly describe this process?**

   A   Novation

   B   Exchange for physical

   C   Physical for exchange

   D   Swap trade

27. **How can the process of price discovery take place on derivatives markets?**

   A   Via a quote driven system

   B   Via an order driven system

   C   Via a quote or order driven system

   D   Via neither a quote or order driven system

28. **Which of the following describes an arbitrage trade?**

   A   Buying a call and buying a put

   B   Buying a call and selling a higher strike call

   C   Buying a call and selling a put while going long the future

   D   Buying the FTSE constituents and selling the FTSE future

29. **Which is the best example of a cross trade?**

   A   A broker buys a security and sells a contract with the same underlying security to his own account

   B   A broker buys a security and sells a contract with the same underlying security to another trader

   C   A broker buys a security and sells a contract with the same underlying security to the house account

   D   A broker buys a security from one client and sells a contract with the same underlying security to another client

30. **You believe the Euro yield curve will invert. Which is the best trade to action?**

   A   Buy 3 Month Euribor Furtures; Buy 10 Year Bund Futures

   B   Buy 3 Month Euribor Furtures; Sell 10 Year Bund Futures

   C   Sell 3 Month Euribor Furtures; Buy 10 Year Bund Futures

   D   Sell 3 Month Euribor Furtures; Sell 10 Year Bund Futures

31. The 500p strike put is priced at 10p; the 460p strike put is priced at 3p. What is the maximum profit on the bear put spread?

   A 7p

   B 33p

   C 13p

   D 47p

32. Why would a speculator sell a horizontal option spread?

   A In anticipation of rising volatility

   B In anticipation of a decline in volatility

   C When interest rates are expected to rise

   D When interest rates are expected to fall

33. What is the name of an option that protects a saver who receives a floating rate over a number of settlement periods?

   A A floor

   B A cap

   C A basement

   D A collar

34. What is the best way of avoiding basis risk?

   A Purchase options to hedge

   B Hold the futures until the delivery date

   C Use the OTC market

   D Lock in the relevant carry costs prior to executing the cash and carry arbitrage

35. What is NOT a correct definition of delta?

   A The absolute change in the price of the option given a change in the price of the underlying

   B The percent change in the price of the option for a 1% change in the price of the underlying

   C The probability of an option expiring in-the-money

   D The proportion of the underlying asset needed to hedge an option

36. Three months ago an investor purchased a call option with a strike of 100p and a March expiry for 12p. If the underlying is now trading at 134p, which of the following most accurately represents his profit or loss?

   A 2p

   B 22p

   C 34p

   D 54p

37.   Which of the following most accurately describes the risk reward profile of a long put?

A   Risk is limited, reward is large but limited

B   Risk is unlimited, reward is unlimited

C   Risk is limited, reward is large but unlimited

D   Risk is unlimited, reward is unlimited

38.   Which of the following is not an example of a risk faced by exchange traded equity option buyers?

A   Liquidity risk

B   Equity risk

C   Interest rate risk

D   Volatility risk?

39.   An investor writes 20 call options on equities (2,000 shares) with a delta of 0.6. How many shares will be have to buy/sell to hedge his exposure?

A   Buy 1,200

B   Sell 1,200

C   Buy 3,333

D   Sell 3,333

40.   A limit order input into LIFFE CONNECT with no cancellation date is presumed to last until when?

A   The end of the trading day

B   Until cancelled

C   Until the end of the contract

D   For five business days after the order is input

41.   To secure an exemption under CFTC Part 30, which of the following must a UK firm do?

A   Register with the FSA

B   Agree to the jurisdiction of the UK courts

C   Join the NFA arbitration scheme

D   Employ only US workers

42.   What strategy would be used by a fund manager seeking to contribute to the cost of acquiring a stock?

A   Covered call

B   Long straddle

C   Long call

D   Long strangle

43. **What kind of strategy involves buying a stock and a put?**

A   Basis trade

B   Intermarket spread

C   A hedge

D   Intramarket spread

---

44. **Why is a pricing factor needed in the long gilt futures contract?**

A   To adjust for differences in the maturity of deliverable gilts

B   To adjust for differences in accrued interest of deliverable gilts

C   To adjust for differences in the prices of deliverable gilts

D   To adjust for differences in the coupon of deliverable gilts

---

45. **Why are give-ups common?**

A   To provide anonymity for proprietary trades

B   To allow trades executed with non-clearing members to clear through LCH.Clearnet

C   As customers frequently use global clearing

D   As most customers have opted out of client money segregation

---

46. **Under what expected market conditions is it best to write a covered call?**

A   Volatile markets

B   When the underlying is expected to rise significantly

C   When the underlying is expected to fall significantly

D   Stable markets

---

47. **The Nikkei 225 is at 10,000 points. The yield is 0.4% and interest rates are at 1%. Calculate the fair value of the 30-day future?**

A   10,005

B   10,050

C   10,060

D   9,950

---

48. **An investor holds a futures contract. Basis risk will occur where the investor also holds a**

A   Cash position in the underlying asset

B   Short futures position in the same contract

C   Long futures position in the same contract with a different delivery date

D   Long call option in the underlying

49. **A firm enters into a basis trade off exchange. What is required to be reported?**

A Price, volume, contract terms and counterparty

B Price, volume and contract terms

C Price and volume

D Price only

50. **Which of the following are true of a Futures and Options Fund?**

    I   It can invest a maximum of 20% into option premium or initial margin

    II   All positions must be fully covered in cash

    III   It is authorised by the FSA

    IV   Examples are tracker funds and guaranteed funds

A I, II and III

B II and III

C II, III, and IV

D I, II, III and IV

51. **Which of the following most correctly describes the cheapest to deliver bond?**

A The bond with the largest value of accrued interest at the delivery date

B The bond with the highest implied repo rate

C The bond with the lowest implied futures price when using the actual market repo rate

D The implied repo rate will always be lower than the market repo rate

52. **What is the name of the US government body that has supervised the securities industry since the Wall Street crash of 1929?**

A IASB

B SEC

C NFA

D FDIC

53. **Which of the following does a UK firm not have comply with to secure exemption under CFTC Part 30?**

A Agree, if sued, to the jurisdiction of the US courts

B Send and receive CFTC risk disclosures back from potential customers

C Join the NFA arbitration scheme

D Treat all monies of US investors as client money, utilizing predetermined netting arrangements across accounts and products

54. Which of these statements is false?

A   The NFA is a self-regulatory organisation

B   The NFA oversees firms operating in the derivatives industry

C   Firms who conduct business with the public must register with the NFA

D   The NFA regulates all markets in the US

55. What is Markit Wire?

A   Markit Wire is a manual on exchange derivatives trade processing system

B   Markit Wire is an automatic on exchange derivatives trade processing system

C   Markit Wire is a manual OTC derivatives trade processing system

D   Markit Wire is an automatic OTC derivatives trade processing system

56. Which of the following is the trade name of the industry owned cooperative that specializes in communicating information via its secure, standardized messaging service?

A   Connect

B   SWIFT

C   BACS

D   CHAPS

57. An investor owns a bond that pays a fixed rate of interest and is redeemable at par. He also has the right but not the obligation to sell the bond back to the issuing company. This type of bond is most commonly known as a

A   Callable bond

B   Puttable bond

C   Tradable bond

D   Convertible bond

58. What is an index linked note?

A   A bond that pays a fixed rate of interest

B   A bond that pays a floating rate of interest with LIBOR as a reference

C   A bond that pays a return based of the performance of an equity index

D   A bond that pays no return at all

59. Which of the following is not one of the activities that make up the clearing process?

A   Executing trades

B   Ensuring trades match

C   Transferring margin from the winners to the losers

D   Ensuring correct quantity and quality of assets at delivery

60. **The following are all terms associated with the process of clearing, except**

   A   Novation

   B   Settlement

   C   Principal to principle structure

   D   Mutual offset system

61. **Which of the following descriptions of an independent guarantee is most accurate?**

   A. It is a guarantee backed by all of the members of the clearing house

   B. It is a guarantee backed by the SEC

   C. It is a guarantee backed by the clearing house alone

   D. It is a guarantee backed by the clearing house and the members of the clearing house

62. **Prime brokers have played an increasingly important role in the hedge fund industry. Which of the following is not a core service that could be expected from a prime broker?**

   A   Securities lending

   B   Operational support

   C   Custodial services

   D   Office space and leasing

63. **Which of the following is not a benefit of an exchange for physical transaction?**

   A   Counterparty credit risk is reduced

   B   Reduced balance sheet and margin requirements due to netting

   C   Margin obligations are eliminated

   D   Can be arranged out of normal market hours

64. **The ability for a firm to act as both agent and principal is known as**

   A   Double capacity

   B   Dual capacity

   C   Twin capacity

   D   Blend capacity

65. **What is the key difference between a total return swap and an asset swap?**

   A   In a total return swap the dividend/interest and capital gain/loss is swapped for a fixed rate. In an asset swap only the dividend/interest is swapped

   B   In a total return swap the dividend/interest and capital gains is not swapped for a fixed rate. In an asset swap only the dividend/interest is swapped

   C   In a total return swap the dividend/interest and capital gains is swapped for a fixed rate. In an asset swap only the dividend/interest is not swapped

   D   In a total return swap the dividend/interest and capital gains is not swapped for a fixed rate. In an asset swap only the dividend/interest is not swapped

66. **What is the key concept underlying the credit derivative market?**

    A Independence

    B Sustainability

    C Isolation

    D Flexibility

67. **Which of the following is an example of a credit event?**

    A Ratings downgrade from AA to BBB

    B A change of senior management

    C An approach from a competitor to merge

    D Filing for bankruptcy

68. **When considering the contents of a master agreement, which of the following would you not expect to be included?**

    A Termination events

    B Rate and day count conventions

    C Events of default

    D Netting arrangements

69. **Which exchange operates a basis trading facility for long gilt futures, STIR futures and Universal stock futures?**

    A NYSE Liffe

    B LME

    C ICE Futures

    D EDX

70. **The credit support annex is used for what?**

    A To detail the framework for collateral provision in an OTC relationship

    B To provide back office support when processing trades

    C To facilitate banks identifying appropriate credit terms

    D To detail the framework for claiming unpaid dues

71. **What is a CDO^2?**

    A A security that is backed by a pool of actual assets

    B A security that is backed by a pool of CDSs

    C A security that is backed by a pool of other CDOs

    D A security that contains an embedded CDS

72. **There are two main processes for determining the value of credit derivatives. What are they?**

    A   The Black Scholes model and binomial pricing model

    B   Interest rate parity and put call parity

    C   The future and forward model

    D   The probability model and the no arbitrage model

73. **Which of the following swaps would be most useful to an investor concerned that the income he was receiving from an equity investment may be at risk?**

    A   Total return swap

    B   Volatility swap

    C   Variance swap

    D   Dividend swap

74. **Which of the following is not an example of an OTC option?**

    A   A look back

    B   A ratchet

    C   A forward

    D   A binary

75. **Which of the following exchanges is incorrectly paired with their clearing house?**

    A   ICE Futures and ICE Clear Europe

    B   One Chicago and CME Clearing/OCC

    C   Eurex and NYMEX Clearing

    D   SGX and SGX - DC

Answers

1. **D** This is the correct definition of a seller's obligations when selling a future

    See Chapter 1, Section 1.1 of your Study Text

2. **B** It is possible to open a futures position in Singapore and close it with a trade in Chicago

    See Chapter 2, Section 3.2 of your Study Text

3. **A** $\text{Delta} = \dfrac{\text{Change in premium}}{\text{Change in price}} = 0.87$

    Change in premium = 0.87 × Change in price (5p)

    Thus, change in premium = 4.35p

    See Chapter 3, Section 2.10 of your Study Text

4. **A** This is the best answer

    See Chapter 3, Section 3.1.3 of your Study Text

5. **B** A broker would be wise to request the collateral before doing any further business

    See Chapter 5, Section 3.2 of your Study Text

6. **D** This is the only accurate description of a forward. The other three are characteristics of a future

    See Chapter 4, Section 1.1 of your Study Text

7. **A** A cap would be the best answer. By purchasing a cap the borrower is effectively buying an option that would give him the right to pay a fixed interest rate on his borrowings once the reference rate moves through a certain level. This is the cap rate

    See Chapter 4, Section 1.3 of your Study Text

8. **C** This is a description of a receiver swaption. The owner will have the right but not the obligation to enter into a swap transaction and receive a fixed rate of interest

    See Chapter 4, Section 1.4.2 of your Study Text

9. **A** The broker has two clients, one who has sold 10 contracts and the other who has bought 10 contracts. The opposite positions are essentially 'flat' in terms of exposure. However if the positions were netted out at the clearing organisation, then the position would not represent the clients' positions exactly. This would cause problems if one client chose to close out or to go to delivery. Therefore, the broker must have the two positions recognised by the clearing house

    See Chapter 5, Section 2.4 of your Study Text

10. **D** Like variation margin, initial margin is due by 09:00 on the following business day

    See Chapter 5, Section 2 of your Study Text

11. **C** We must start with the seller deciding when, what and where exactly they wish to deliver under the permitted settlement terms of the contract. This will then be randomly matched with an open long position. LCH.Clearnet must have calculated the invoice amount before the settlement can occur

See Chapter 2, Section 3 of your Study Text

12. **D** Remember it is only General Clearing Members that can clear for the firm, its clients and other investment businesses

See Chapter 5, Section 1.1.1 of your Study Text

13. **D** $$\frac{\$30m}{1425 \times \$500}$$

Therefore, sell 42 contracts

See Chapter 6, Section 4.3 of your Study Text

14. **C** This is the best answer. The other options all relate to the TCF framework

See Chapter 7, Section 1.2 of your Study Text

15. **B** The Securities and Exchange Commission and Commodities Future Trading Commission is the best answer

See Chapter 7, Sections 2.2 and 2.3 of your Study Text

16. **C** Remember straddles use call and put options with the same strike. Spread are created using all calls or all puts

See Chapter 6, Section 3.7.4 of your Study Text

17. **C** Both Futures and Options Funds and Geared Futures and Options Funds are Regulated Collective Investment schemes and must be authorized

See Chapter 6, Section 7.5 of your Study Text

18. **C** Since the investor manages the account himself he does not need to pay fees to a professional money manager

See Chapter 6, Section 7.2 of your Study Text

19. **D** The definition is very broad and includes instruments whose value has been in whole or in part determined directly or indirect by reference to an underlying security

See Chapter 7, Section 4 of your Study Text

20. **C** International Accounting Standard 39 – Financial Instruments – Recognition and measurement details the framework for accounting for derivatives in financial statements. Its main focus is that all derivative transactions should be included at fair value in the accounts, unless they are specifically for hedging purposes when they can be included at book value

See Chapter 7, Section 4.3 of your Study Text

21. **A** The cash price is trading well above the futures price implying strong demand in the cash market. This will occur when there is a "short squeeze" and traders need to buy the cash commodity to make delivery on short futures contracts

See Chapter 3, Section 1.5 of your Study Text

22. **B** There is no need to include the counterparty details when determining implied volatility. The complete list of inputs include underlying price, strike price, interest rates, time to expiry and market price of option

See Chapter 3, Section 2.5 of your Study Text

23. **A** This describes the fact that initial margin takes into account a member's overall position. Therefore should the risk on the new contracts be offset by any other existing positions, the amount of margin payable will be reduced accordingly

See Chapter 5, Section 2.6.3 of your Study Text

24. **D** This is a vertical bull spread with calls. With a bull spread you buy the low strike and sell the high strike. This spread trade results in an initial debit of 4 (-8 + 4), this means the maximum loss is 4. The maximum gain is the difference in between the strikes 106 - 100 = 6 minus the initial debit of 4 = 2

See Chapter 6, Section 3.3 of your Study Text

25. **B** Simply use the formula: Call – Put = Equity and rearrange:

Put = Equity – Call (i.e. Synthetic short put = Long equity and short call)

See Chapter 6, Section 3.2 of your Study Text

26. **B** An exchange for physical or EFP is a transaction in which the buyer of a cash commodity transfers to the seller a corresponding amount of long futures contracts or receives from the seller a corresponding amount of short futures

See Chapter 1, Section 3.1.2 of your Study Text

27. **C** For derivatives markets, price discovery is generated though two different types of market systems. A quote-driven market is one where prices are determined my designated market makers or dealers. This is sometimes described as a 'price driven' market. An order driven market is one where the buy and sell orders placed in the trading system result in the best bid price and lowest sell price, resulting in a transaction taking place

See Chapter 1, Section 4.3 of your Study Text

28. **D** This is a cash and carry arbitrage. The reversal arbitrage involves creating a synthetic long by buying a call and selling a put, but it is then necessary to SELL the future. Remember the future must always be traded in the same direction as the put in an arbitrage trade

See Chapter 3, Section 1.6 of your Study Text

29. **D** Answer D describes "effecting a cross" where a broker buys a security from one client and sells it to another client earning two sets of commission

See Chapter 3, Section 4.1 of your Study Text

30. **C** If you believe the yield curve will invert you expect long term interest rates to fall relative to short rates and therefore bond futures prices to rise

See Chapter 6, Section 2.2 of your Study Text

31. **B** Remember with the bear spread you always sell the low strike (and buy the high strike). Therefore you are spending 7p in net premium and this is therefore a debit trade and the net premium must be your maximum loss. The maximum profit is therefore simply the difference in strikes (40p) less the premium you spent (7p)

See Chapter 6, Section 3.3 of your Study Text

32. **A** Selling a horizontal spread means selling the short dated option and buying the long dated option of the same type (i.e. both calls or both puts) and at the same strike. An increase in volatility will have more impact on the longer dated option and therefore this trade will be profitable if volatility goes up. (The short dated option is sold to neutralise the effect of a movement up or down in the price of the underlying)

See Chapter 6, Section 3.1.1 of your Study Text

33. **A** A floor is a series of put options that allow the saver to receive a fixed rate. The holder would exercise the right if funds fall below the pre-determined floor level. Caps protect floating rate borrowers such that the borrower never pays more than the cap rate. A collar is a combination of a cap and a floor. The strategy involves buying one and selling the other. Strikes are normally chosen such that the premiums offset each other, i.e. there is **nil** net cost. Basement is used as a distractor.

See Chapter 4, Section 1.3 of your Study Text

34. **B** Basis is defined as Cash price – Futures price. At delivery the cash price and futures price are the same and there is no further basis risk. This process is known as convergence

See Chapter 3, Section 1.5 of your Study Text

35. **B** Delta is a ratio of absolute amounts not a percentage

See Chapter 3, Section 2.10 of your Study Text

36. **B** The buying of a call option is known as a long call. The investor is motivated by the view the underlying asset price will move and he will be able to exercise his option to buy the asset at a price below the underlying price and therefore make a profit. However, any profits and losses must considered alongside the original cost of the option or premium. In this example, the profit on exercise would be 134p less the strike of 100p. But we must also subtract the cost of the option giving us a net profit of 22p

See Chapter 1, Section 1.11 of your Study Text

37. **A** This is the correct description of a long put's risk reward profile

See Chapter 1, Section 1.13 of your Study Text

38. **A** A buyer of an exchange traded equity option will not suffer from any liquidity risk as he will be able to sell the option back into the exchange. Liquidity risk would only arise if the transaction occurred off the exchange of OTC

See Chapter 1, Section 1.18 of your Study Text

39. **A** The investor will have to buy 2,000 × 0.6 = 1,200

See Chapter 3, Section 2.10 of your Study Text

40. **A** The default assumption is that orders last until the end of the trading day

See Chapter 3, Section 4.2.2 of your Study Text

41. **C** This is one of the six requirements for access to the scheme

See Chapter 7, Section 2.4.1 of your Study Text

42. **A** A covered call involves being long shares and selling call options on those shares. The premium received for selling the calls will reduce the net cost of acquiring the shares

See Chapter 6, Section 8.1 of your Study Text

43. **C** Buying a put option will hedge the downside risk of the shares

See Chapter 6, Section 5.2 of your Study Text

44. **C** The pricing factor reflects differences in the relative cash prices of the deliverable gilts compared to a hypothetical 6% 10-year gilt. These relative prices are in turn influenced by the coupon and maturity

See Chapter 6, Section 4.1.1 of your Study Text

45. **C** Derivative customers that are heavy users of derivatives may split their business among different brokers but elect a single global clearer for operational efficiency. Allocations or give-ups are used to pass all the trades executed with different brokers to the single global clearer. Screen based trading is always anonymous – it is only in open outcry trading that give-ups may be used for anonymity

See Chapter 3, Section 5.2 of your Study Text

46. **D** A covered call is an effective strategy when the market is stable. If you are long an asset in a static market then you will not be able to increase the value of your portfolio by just sitting on the position. You create a covered call by selling call options and benefiting from the incoming premium. The premise is that the short calls will not be exercised since the market is static. Should the market actually rise and the call options be exercised then you are long the asset so are covered

See Chapter 6, Section 8.1 of your Study Text

47. **A** The theoretical value of the future = cash price plus carry costs (interest rate – dividend yield)

10,000 x (0.006 × 30/365) + 10,000 = 10,005

See Chapter 3, Section 1.3 of your Study Text

48. **A** Basis is defined as cash price – futures price. Basis risk arises when an investor holds a cash position and an offsetting futures position, e.g. long cash and short future or vice versa

See Chapter 3, Section 1.5 of your Study Text

49. **B**   When trade reporting you do not have to report the counterparty to the trade. This would, however, be required for transaction reporting

See Chapter 3, Section 3.1 of your Study Text

50. **C**   Futures and Options funds are Regulated Collective Investment Schemes and authorised by the FSA. All positions must be covered in cash and a maximum of 10% is permitted to be used to pay initial margin or option premium. They are called synthetic or tracker funds when they invest in futures or guaranteed funds when they purchase options

See Chapter 6, Section 7.5 of your Study Text

51   **B**   The correct answer will always be that the cheapest to deliver bond is the one with the highest implied repo rate

See Chapter 6, Section 4.1.2 of your Study Text

52.   **B**   The Securities and Exchange Commission is the best answer. The IASB is an accounts standards setting body, the NFA is a self regulating body with specific focus on futures and the FDIC is the body responsible for insuring deposits held at banks in the US

See Chapter 7, Section 2.2 of your Study Text

53.   **D**   UK firms must agree to treat all monies as client money without netting them off under any netting arrangements. It is possible to opt out of this rule, but that is only for more sophisticated investors. Generally no netting off is allowed

See Chapter 7, Section 2.4 of your Study Text

54.   **D**   Markets in the US are regulated by the SEC and the CFTC

See Chapter 7, Sections 2.2 and 2.3 of your Study Text

55.   **D**   Answer D is the correct description of Markit Wire

See Chapter 4, Section 6.1 of your Study Text

56.   **B**   SWIFT is the industry owned messaging service that connects over 8,000 institutions in 208 countries around the world

See Chapter 4, Section 6.4 of your Study Text

57.   **B**   This is a puttable bond

See Chapter 4, Section 4.4 of your Study Text

58.   **C**   This is the best description of an index linked note

See Chapter 4, Section 4.2 of your Study Text

59.   **A**   Trade execution is not part of the clearing process. The other three activities are

See Chapter 5, Section 1.1 of your Study Text

60.   **B**   Settlement is the process of exchanging legal title and is the last stage of any transaction's life span. It is normally associated with cash products but can also be associated with derivatives. All of the other terms are specifically to do with clearing

See Chapter 5, Section 1.2 of your Study Text

61. **C** An independent guarantee is one which is backed by the resources of the clearing house alone. The alternative, which is used by LCH, is a mutual guarantee structure, whereby the clearing members will share any losses incurred

See Chapter 5, Section 1.3 of your Study Text

62. **D** Office space and leasing is not a core service but instead is referred to as a value added service

See Chapter 5, Section 1.6 of your Study Text

63. **C** By exchanging an OTC or cash position for a futures position, we are bringing an off exchange transaction onto the exchange. As a result margin will be required by the clearing house. Answer C is therefore not a benefit of EFP transactions

See Chapter 2, Section 2.5 of your Study Text

64. **B** The ability to act as agent and principle is known as dual capacity

See Chapter 2, Section 1.1 of your Study Text

65. **A** A tricky question. A is the best answer of the four and accurately describes the main distinction between a total return swap and an asset swap

See Chapter 4, Section 1.8 of your Study Text

66. **C** The key concept underlying the credit market is isolation. Consequently the buyer of a credit derivative wants to isolate the credit risk of an underlying asset from other key risks such as FX risk or interest rate risk

See Chapter 4, Section 1.9 of your Study Text

67. **D** Filing for bankruptcy is an example of a credit event. Others include, failure to meet debt repayment obligations, restructuring and a repudiation as a result in the change in ownership of an asset

See Chapter 4, Section 1.9 of your Study Text

68. **B** Rate and day count conventions would implicit in the terms of the transaction and would therefore be located on the term sheet not the master agreement

See Chapter 4, Section 2.1 of your Study Text

69. **A** NYSE Liffe provides a basis trading facility. This allows for the simultaneous purchase or sale of a bond in the cash market and offsetting purchases in the futures market without using the exchanges dealing systems

See Chapter 2, Section 2.4 of your Study Text

70. **A** The credit support annex is one of the four documents that make up the master agreement. It is not mandatory and details the framework for providing credit support or collateral provision in OTC transactions

See Chapter 4, Section 2.2 of your Study Text

71. **C** A CDO^2 is a security that invests in other CDOs. It is a similar in concept to a fund of funds investment. The other options refer to different securities. A refers to a CDO, B to a synthetic CDO and D refers to a credit linked note

See Chapter 4, Section 3.1 of your Study Text

72. **D** The probability and no arbitrage models are two alternative models used by the market to price credit derivatives

See Chapter 4, Section 3.2 of your Study Text

73. **D** A dividend swap is specifically used by investors who are looking to swap away dividend payments from stocks. By swapping the dividends in exchange for a fixed payment, the investor effectively eliminates the risk the dividend is cut or is lower then expected

See Chapter 4, Section 3.3.3 of your Study Text

74. **C** A forward is a financial instrument that defers delivery or receipt of an underlying asset. All of the others are examples of OTC options

See Chapter 4, Section 5 of your Study Text

75. **C** Eurex is cleared using the Eurex Clearing AG

See Chapter 5, Section 1.7 of your Study Text